Dear Daughter
by Wil LaVeist, PhD.

© Copyright 2020 Wil LaVeist, PhD.

ISBN 978-1-63393-461-0

All rights reserved. No part of this publication may be reproduced, stored in a retrieval system, or transmitted in any form or by any means – electronic, mechanical, photocopy, recording, or any other – except for brief quotations in printed reviews, without the prior written permission of the author.

First published by Köehler Books 2017

Published by

110 Coliseum Crossing
Suite 316
Hampton, VA 23666
www.willaveist.com

Dear Daughter

*A dad's marriage advice to women on
love, pain, healing and the law*

Wil LaVeist

Table of Contents

Introduction

Chapter 1: Get to Know Yourself First 7

Chapter 2: Warning Signs—You Get What You See 27

Chapter 3: Premarital Counseling 45

Chapter 4: Why it's NOT Cheaper to Keep Her (or Him) 54

Chapter 5: Your Life Will No Longer Be Your Own—Can You Handle That? 69

Chapter 6: The Power of Empathy 79

Chapter 7: How to Prepare for Marriage in the Divorce Age 88

Chapter 8: Pre-Marital Divorce Advice 97

Chapter 9: Advice from Marriage Reality Veterans 128

Chapter 10: THE QUIZ—Are You Ready for Marriage? 141

Conclusion 148

Acknowledgments

DEAR DAUGHTER

INTRODUCTION

During my divorce after 21 years of marriage, I uncovered a truth that dropped me and my daughter to our knees. I learned that my now adult daughter—my baby girl—is NOT my biological child. The daughter whose umbilical cord I had cut as I caressed her in a blanket against my chest. The daughter whom I had taken on her first date to the daddy/daughter dance at elementary school. The daughter that I drove to college and helped to move into her dorm room for her freshman year away from home.

My only daughter.

A chance paternity test uncovered the truth. When I opened the envelope and saw the DNA results reading "Probability of Paternity 0%," I was floored. It was as if my apartment spun in painful slow motion. It was the darkest moment of my life to date. Then, three months later that darkness turned pitch black. After a second paternity test that confirmed the first result, I had to finally tell my daughter the horrible truth. As we sat in my car and wiped each other's tears, I saw a deep sorrow in her eyes that I had never witnessed. I pray that I never see such sorrow in her or anyone ever again.

But through my deep pain also came a sense of clarity and even relief. So much of what I had suspected about my *so-called marriage*, but had not fully understood, came into focus. The root of the frustrating behavior I endured began to make sense. I thought to myself, "Show me a woman who missed being nurtured and protected by her father, and I'll show you a wife who will lash out against her husband. Show me a woman who has not resolved or at least confronted her own 'daddy issues,' and I'll show you a mother who will inevitably wound her own children."

"*Dear Daughter,*" is a love letter from a father (me) to his daughter to empower her to become a healthy woman who can handle a successful love relationship and marriage. This book is particularly for women who are considering marriage and having children. After all, in America, marriage remains the ideal relationship under which children are often born and, unfortunately, issues of paternity and broken relationships occur. The book contains the information that I want my daughter to know about love and relationships to help her to create her own much healthier family if she chooses to become a wife and mother.

The book, in the tangible form of words on pages, embodies the loving relationship that my daughter and I have maintained since she was a baby. She is a classic "daddy's girl," and I'm the adoring dad. But, ironically, my daughter now faces potential "daddy issues" like many young women whose fathers are not in their lives—issues imposed upon them by someone else. My hope is that through our father/daughter bond remaining strong, that the stunning reality of our genetic brokenness will not drive her to personal disarray or denial. I want her (and other women) to understand that if she does not confront her "daddy issues" she WILL have relationship problems. Inevitably she will wound her husband, and even worse, her innocent children.

Ironically, I have been blessed to be a "father to many." Close friends of my daughter and sons, while growing up, also call me "Dad"—particularly my daughter's friends who have not had healthy relationships with their fathers. This book is written to them also, as well as the many women who have been wounded to help them to NOT pass on their pain to their loved ones. This realization became crystal clear to me when I was asked to speak at a Baltimore, Maryland area workshop for women who had been wounded by their fathers. I shared my story to help them to heal. Their overwhelmingly positive response helped ME to heal. The experience helped to shape this book.

When fathers wound their daughters, the consequences are often far-reaching for generations. Fathers are key to giving daughters a positive sense of identity, self-love and security that they will need as women and potentially wives and mothers. Fathers are vital to helping shape their daughters' views of men. These are the roots of "daddy issues." When a father fails to pass these keys on to his daughter, and if the daughter in turn fails to take accountability for her "daddy issues" and actions as an adult woman, she WILL lash out at her husband. If she becomes a mother, she WILL pass down her pain to her own children, particularly her daughter for whom she is the primary role model. Sons are obviously not immune to daddy (or mommy) issues. If the father is absent, or is present but dysfunctional, the chain of pain will pass to the son also. Ultimately, wounded children grow up to become wounded adults who create dysfunctional relationships, marriages, families, and so on, and so on . . .

Two decades of matrimony ought to teach a person something about what it takes for a healthy couple's partnership to work. To get off of my "un-merry-go-'round" relationship, I had finally come to grips with the fact that the so-called marriage hadn't been working and never would. To many observers, my marriage and family appeared to be healthy. "Oh, what a lovely couple," people would say. "You guys with your three great children are like an all-American TV family." However, the reality of the so-called perfect marriage and family is that it doesn't exist! TV families aren't real and the actors are often dysfunctional and flawed in their private lives. Reality TV is scripted. For too many American families, including my family of five, the appearance of perfection is often a smokescreen for deep pains and sins—known and unknown.

In America, where the average marriage lasts about three to five years, the longevity of my union was enough to convince many friends and associates that I had found the secret to "making it work." But like many people I know, I should have never said, "I do" in the first place. I had glossed over the deal-breaking signs that we were obviously NOT "the ones" for each other. Many of my family members and close friends were saddened but not shocked about the breakup. However, none of them saw coming the shocking truth concerning my daughter's paternity. Now at this point, if you are considering getting married, you might be thinking, "Why would I want to take marriage advice from a divorced (or technically divorced) man?" Please, keep reading.

Dear Daughter illustrates the type of pain-saving wisdom that many women miss out on when their father/daughter relationship is broken or nonexistent. The book shows that most couples are trying to make work a marriage that needed much more preparation and evaluation BEFORE saying "I do." It addresses some warning signs to heed to avoid winding up with the wrong person and much more. While the personal stories in the book are written from the perspective of a middle-aged heterosexual man—that's who I am and what I know—there is also much here for people considering a same-sex marriage. At least two of my daughter's friends—my "additional daughters"—are openly gay. All readers will learn that, unlike the message in the classic 1970s song, "Cheaper to Keep Her," it's not always cheaper—emotionally or financially—to stay in a relationship—with a woman or a man—that has no hope of fulfillment. And believe me, as a veteran of a long marriage that had its troubles even before the knot was officially tied, I know what I'm talking about. This book offers advice for those who are considering marrying for the first time or remarrying. It will help you discover who you are and to be honest about what you want in a marriage partner. It will help you to avoid being the object of someone else's pain, or worse—passing on your pain to your innocent child.

Over the course of a more than 25-year print, online and broadcast journalism career, I've been blessed to interview and mingle with a variety of people all over the country and abroad who are of different races, ethnicities and social classes. I've been privy to some of the most intimate details of their lives. In more recent years, on my radio show and podcast, *The Wil LaVeist Show*, which originates from Hampton, Virginia, guests have spoken about their marriage trials, and relationship experts have doled out advice to listeners. A guest who was adopted by a loving married couple shared the trials of her 35-year quest to find her biological parents. While altered to obscure their identities, the stories here are based on my subjects', friends' and acquaintances' collective experiences and personal anecdotes.

Advice comes from me and relationship professionals. My citing and quoting of certain experts does not mean nor imply that they endorse my views expressed in this book.

The shocking truth I received about my daughter's paternity during my divorce certainly floored me. Later in the book, I recount in detail the moment I opened the envelope and read the paternity results. I discuss the Virginia judge and his puzzling contradictory divorce ruling. I discuss why antiquated paternity fraud laws should be changed so that the guilty are held accountable and the innocent—particularly the child—are able to obtain legal justice. (As a result of my meeting with a member of the Virginia General Assembly, a senate bill was introduced in 2017). Uncovering the truth that I am not my daughter's biological father has been by far the darkest moment of my life. Darker than being blindsided by a firing, which led me to write my award-winning book *Fired Up*. Darker than facing the death of my mother. However, this is not a "woe is me" diatribe. I remain pro marriage! And I will always be pro daughters—especially my daughter.

CHAPTER 1
GET TO KNOW YOURSELF FIRST

My Wonderful Daughter,

It seems like just the other day that I would stand over your crib in the middle of the night just after you were born. I would feed you before heading to my newspaper job on the 3 a.m. copy desk. Before heading out the bedroom door, I would marvel at your beauty as you drifted back to sleep. Now in your mid-20s, I am so proud of the young woman that you have evolved into. Do you still remember what I would always tell you while you were growing up? That it's not how pretty you are on the outside, but how pretty you are on the inside that counts most? I had no idea of the deeper meaning that my words would hold for us as father and daughter now that we know the painful truth after so many years.

You are coming into your own as a woman now. Your identity is critical. Despite the challenge of the identity of your biological father, you must never lose your sense of self, *even along your complex journey to personal discovery. Don't even think about getting married, blending your life with the goals and dreams of another person, if you haven't become confident in knowing yourself first. The root cause of many failed marriages goes back to this one simple yet major mistake people make: thinking marriage will help them put their problems and issues in the past, and that another person will be the elixir to most, if not all that ails them. Listen: You've got to take responsibility for getting yourself "right" on your own terms before you get married—in fact, before you get involved in a major relationship, period. You likely won't resolve all of your issues (and you're not alone—everyone has issues), but it's imperative that you put the major ones to rest and that you continue working on yourself.*

I call these issues "unpacked luggage." These are the major unresolved hurts, insecurities, pet peeves, bad habits and the like that people drag around throughout their lives. When you arrive home after a long trip, what do you do? You unpack your luggage, right? In a marriage, you'll unpack the suitcases of your past when you get home with your mate and the smell of your dirty laundry will fill the room. And even after you've done the work to get to know your own self, inevitably you'll still bring some of your luggage to a relationship. But one thing's for sure: You can vow to deal with your soiled clothes before you get involved with someone. You need to first know clearly what's in your own bags before you embark on what would be a lifetime of handling your soul mate's issues, too. But most of all, my daughter, by confronting your issues, you can significantly decrease the chances that you'll pass on your pain to your mate and children. Your dad is with you. I will always have your back. I love you unconditionally.

This chapter will explore some of the types of issues you should work on before entering a relationship, and will provide tips and tools to help you do your own internal work first to heal, whether you work on it with a counselor (which I highly recommend) or do it yourself. This will help you to be better aware of what's going on in your own head, and to avoid pairing up with a person who's wrong for you. If you have a better sense of who you are as an individual, what you want in a relationship, and where you're going in life, you will be able to project these into the universe instead of unknowingly projecting what you DON'T want. What you project out into the universe—whether desirable or undesirable—will return to you, so project wisely.

LAW OF ATTRACTION: Like Attracts Like

The law of attraction is a concept that says, like a magnet, we draw people and circumstances to ourselves based on the energy that we project into the universe. It works whether you dispatch positive or negative energy. The law is believed to work just like any of the other laws of the universe; for example, the law of gravity: If you toss something up, it will certainly fall down. Though there is no scientific proof to the law of attraction, there are many who believe in it. Author James Allen elaborated on it in his classic 1902 book, *As a Man Thinketh*:

> *Mind is the Master power that moulds and makes,*
> *And Man is Mind, and evermore he takes*
> *The tool of Thought, and, shaping what he wills,*
> *Brings forth a thousand joys, a thousand ills:*
> *He thinks in secret, and it comes to pass:*
> *Environment is but his looking-glass.*

Clearly "woman" (the man with the womb) is included in Allen's use of the term man, meaning "humans." Marriage is definitely about what's in the minds of two people and the union created from their thoughts. As Allen wrote, and I paraphrase a bit here, the environment is but your looking-glass.

So back to resolving your issues and how the law of attraction relates to it and a successful, or far too often, unsuccessful marriage. For example, if you were traumatized by a parent as a child, you will likely attract a person who is like that parent. Perhaps they'll look like your parent or share certain personality traits with them. This potential partner will provide an opportunity for you to possibly get a "do-over" of your relationship from childhood—to right the wrong that you endured. You don't let on to this during the dating phase, because that's typically when people keep their dirty laundry hidden in order to put their best faces forward. But after you've exchanged marriage vows, you feel free to take the mask off and unpack. If you had issues with your mother, for instance, because you and your siblings have different biological fathers, it's a good chance that your mate will find himself or herself feeling your wrath if you didn't resolve that issue with your mom. So much of this happens on a subconscious level, which is why we often fail to see it coming and happening until it's up on us and too late.

I highly recommend professional counseling, especially if you know you've experienced a trauma. (I'll go into more detail about counseling and other ways to get to know yourself and work on resolving your issues later in the chapter.) A sign of your problem could be that you've had trouble maintaining past relationships. If you're the common denominator in your dysfunctional love pairings, chances are that your luggage has been getting in the way. On a personal level, I know this all too well.

UNPACKED LUGGAGE: MY OWN STORY

A few years into my marriage, I began feeling that it would not last long-term. We kept going 'round and 'round unhappily on the same disagreements revolving around trust and shared vision. So I began thinking about divorce. My family lived in the Chicago area then. About seven years in, I nearly pulled the trigger after a major crisis, but agreed to do marriage counseling instead with our pastor and his wife. Counseling BEFORE marrying would have been better. I thought it best to keep our family intact. My pastor and good friend, bless his heart (and his metaphor), convinced me to keep, "Watering your plant."

"You chose the plant (your wife), so now you need to take care of it and keep it healthy," he would say.

Brother Pastor loves his metaphors and acronyms! To this day, though I no longer live in Illinois, my pastor remains one of my closest confidants, and his wife is like a sister from another mother. So after we moved to Virginia, I kept on watering. As a consequence, I kept on keeping on as a married man. Then, about 13 years into our union, I remember stumbling upon "The Unexpected Legacy of Divorce: Report of a 25-Year Study." It was an eye-opener that provided additional insight into my marriage problems carousel.

The study, published in 2004, is about the effects that divorce has on children. Being a product of divorced parents, it definitely caught my attention. Researchers Judith S. Wallerstein and Julia M. Lewis tracked 131 children ages 3 to 18 whose parents divorced in the 1970s. They wanted to see how things turned out for the subjects in terms of their relationships, marriages, and rearing of children. The researchers compared their results to a similar control group of children who were from intact families. What they found was that children of divorced parents tended to have more problems than those whose parents had stayed together. For example, of the people who were tracked, they found that one in five of the girls had their first sexual experience before age 14. These girls were growing up without their fathers and missing their dad's attention. They sought the attention from other males. Though sex wasn't their main goal, it became a consequence of the relationship. Also, pregnancy was a likely result because precautions were usually not taken.

The researchers also reported that children of divorced parents used drugs more heavily and more often, and that once these children became adults, the trauma of divorce often had a significant impact on their ability to love and trust in their own adult relationships.

Being from divorced parents was always a major motivator for me to remain married. I didn't want my children to experience the pain I had endured. Growing up in the late 1970s and 1980s, I saw the change in my neighborhood, where more and more families were splitting up as legislation was enacted to make no-fault divorces easier to obtain. I remember being around 9 years old and playing an electronic football game (yeah, this is *waaaay* before Madden NFL video games) with one of my friends at my home. My parents broke out into an argument, embarrassing me. My friend said something like, "Don't worry, man. My mom and dad do the same thing."

By age 12, when my parents divorced, I was in full trauma mode though I didn't know it then. I lashed out and began getting poor grades in middle school. I got into a lot of fights. I used drugs and alcohol to medicate, which unfortunately was the norm for kids growing up in my tough, stressful Brooklyn neighborhood. But thankfully I was a very good athlete. In playing baseball, basketball and football, I found a safer release and focus that helped to ease my pain. Also, that my two older brothers and one sister that I was raised with (I have three older sisters in all) had modeled success by moving out to attend college was huge. My oldest brother, Greg, graduated as the most outstanding male student of his class. As he delivered his speech on stage, I remember watching him and thinking, "Well, I know I'll at least graduate from college." It was a tough journey, but through many prayers and much support, including from my father, who remained consistently involved, things turned around and I found my own correct path.

The findings of the Wallerstein and Lewis study, which were consistent with my experiences, were sobering for me to understand the effect that my parents' divorce had had on me and my love relationships. Of course, many children from divorced parents grow up to do fine and have healthy love pairings, but I was not one of them. There were several other interesting findings in the report, but as I read, certain passages began to catch my attention more deeply. For example, this one:

> "Over half of our subjects reported memory fragments that captured key moments of the breakup or the years that followed. These images intruded into their adult relationships at crisis

> points. One woman in her 30s told us that her strongest memory of her parents' divorce, when she was 11 years old, was of her father crying as he walked slowly down the flower-bordered path away from the family home, after her mom threw him out because of his adultery. This memory flashed before her eyes whenever she contemplated leaving her alcoholic boyfriend. By her account, her boyfriend's tears brought back the image of her weeping father and prevented her from leaving. Such fragments, which so frequently loomed large in their adult relationships, reflected the suffering of the parent that the child had perceived and internalized. The rawness of the parental suffering following the breakup left an indelible emotional mark. One woman said, 'I could never do to another human being what my mother did to my father.' We found that more than half of our subjects carried similar memory fragments, which became powerful intruders into their adult relationships. The child's lasting internalizing of the parent's suffering or joy has largely been unrecognized."

Reading this, I recalled when my mother brought me to the courthouse during her and my father's divorce proceeding. I don't think I had a clue where I was going. As I walked through the building's corridor, the courtroom doors reminded me of being in the school hallway approaching one of my classrooms. Outside the courtroom, my mother had me sit on a bench along the wall. As I did, my father walked from down the hall toward me. Beside him was a guy wearing a suit and tie. My father did a double-take and then our eyes locked. I saw a glimpse of despair in his face. (At the time of this writing, Pop is 92 and he STILL remembers this painful moment vividly!) I was confused. Their marriage mess that had nothing to do with me. I had no idea that it would affect me for years to come. Court is no place for a kid.

As I continued reading the study, another passage gripped me:

"Hardly any of our subjects described a happy childhood; in fact, a number of children told us that 'the day they divorced was the day my childhood ended.' Older children took on a lot of responsibility in the household, taking care of younger children and often taking care of needy parents as well. They were proud of their helpful role and developed compassion and a sense of moral responsibility at an early age. For those who did too much over too many years, the price was high. They lost out on their childhood and adolescent pleasures and important aspects of their social development. A discovery at the 25-year mark was how frequently they installed the familiar caregiving role into their own adult relationships, and how often they sought out needy, troubled partners whom they nurtured to their own emotional detriment."

"Ding, ding, ding!!!" The alarm clock in my head finally went off.

Staring back at me in each word on the page was myself in many of my relationships with women. Many times in a relationship, you may want to blame your partner for why things aren't going as you planned. But oftentimes, it's really about what's going on with YOU. Besides, YOU are the only one whose behavior YOU can change! As a child of divorced parents, I began to realize that I had some extra hurdles to overcome. Not only did I have a dysfunctional model to refer to, but more importantly, I had to realize how deeply I was affected by what happened AFTER my parents' divorce. I had developed the "needy gene!" I was a codependent.

Different childhood issues can lead to various relationship inadequacies in adulthood. Codependency is one, and I'll address it first and at length, but other issues also include, but are not limited to, trust issues that are linked to your attachment style, and the notion that love is pain. Let's explore these issues.

CODEPENDENCY

Codependency Syndrome refers to a relationship where a person is controlled or manipulated by another person. The manipulator typically has a pathological condition such as Narcissistic Personality Syndrome or an addiction. Codependency was initially associated with people in relationships with alcoholics or drug addicts. However, it's now commonly understood that, if, for example, you have an ill parent or loved one that you have been taking care of for years, chances are you are codependent. The person that you've been caring for does not necessarily have to be a negative or destructive personality. They could be a younger sibling who has a special need and who is actually an inspiration to the family. However, the process of taking care of that person can condition you to become a codependent.

After my parents divorced, my late mother went through a lot of tough financial times and personal challenges. She had a stroke when I was around 16 years old. I thought she was going to die. After school, I would travel for an hour on the city bus to feed her at home and then return to school for football practice. For many years she was bitter toward my father about how her life had turned out. Meanwhile, he remarried and got on with his life. His second marriage has lasted well beyond his (as my mom would often proclaim in her distinct Spanish accent) *"twenty-one plus yeeeears"* first marriage. At the time of this writing, Pop is still going strong with his devoted wife! I felt the void of his absence in the home, though he remained very active and present in my life. Before I left for college at age 18, I lived with my mother the longest through these trying times as my siblings moved out to make their way in the world. I heard Mom cry often. I heard Mom curse often. I witnessed Mom's pain.

Now, my experience with my mother was by no means all negative. I also witnessed Mom make smart moves to push forward with her life as best she could. For example, she finally got her finances together and we moved to a better neighborhood. I saw her join organizations and develop a different social circle beyond the one she and my father had been associated with even prior to their marriage.

Mom was witty, often fun to be around, and had a zest for life. An old school Dominican Latina who was among the first wave of brave legal immigrants to the United States in the 1940s, she was passionate and loved to sing and dance. She was highly intelligent and an avid reader (she wrote and spoke fluently in English and Spanish) and could discuss or debate current events and politics with the best. At the dinner table, we discussed a lot of things about life in general. Through our close relationship, I became more sensitive to and respectful of a woman's point of view on a variety of matters. But through all of this, I was still a kid who was being conditioned to be a caregiver (codependent) for an adult. I was dealing with adult problems in a way that subconsciously created in me an "I can fix you" mindset. And this would eventually play out in my own codependent intimate relationships with women.

From high school through college and after graduation, my friends and family would often be puzzled by the amount of energy and attention I would give to certain young women companions who seemed to have a lot of baggage. They would say things such as, "Why are you with this one who brings all of that stress and drama and confusion to your life, when you can easily be with that one over there who is calm and who really cares for you?" My response would be, "I don't know what you're talking about."

The truth is, I really didn't know! What they were seeing play out before their eyes were issues that were flowing deep inside my head. They were seeing my dominant subconscious mind seeking out relationships with women whom I *mistakenly perceived* to be in need of remedies that I, and apparently, only I could provide. That "needy gene" was acting out.

Codependency is actually very common. It is often referred to as having that "Knight in Shining Armor Syndrome" or savior complex. In heterosexual relationships, the woman is looking for someone to protect them, take care of them, and tell them what to do, while the "Mr. Fix-It Guy" wearing the shining armor wants to oblige. The syndrome also grips codependent "Ms. Fix It" women. In case you didn't know, there are many men out there who are looking for women to be their sponsors. These men oftentimes have been traumatized as children and so they (knowing or unknowingly) attract women for medication.

Do you know of a guy who just doesn't seem to be able to keep a steady job, so he's living off of you? How about the guy who keeps threatening to hurt himself every time his woman talks about leaving the relationship?

The Human Magnet Syndrome: Why We Love People Who Hurt Us by Ross Rosenberg is a powerful book about codependent pairings. In a 2012 essay, Rosenberg describes what he calls the dysfunctional "codependency dance" where two opposite partners attract each other into an unhealthy relationship. He writes:

> "As natural followers in their relationship 'dance,' codependents are passive and accommodating dance partners. Codependents find narcissistic dance partners deeply appealing as they are perpetually attracted to their charm, boldness, confidence and domineering personality."

This sounds like extremely heavy, crazy stuff that no one in their right mind would want to admit being associated with; but having a syndrome does not mean that you are crazy. It would be understandable if the initial reaction to Rosenberg's description of a codependent was, "Heck, that's not me," but I have no doubt that this description of being a codependent is true for many people. However, the challenge of figuring out how to apply good academic research to your life is that researchers often showcase extremes to make their point of what the tendencies of the syndrome are. The important thing to understanding is that most conditions or syndromes exist in varying degrees, and that you should explore to what degree you might be individually affected. You may not fit perfectly into the description, but don't be fooled—there's likely a lot of you there!

As for me being a codependent, in none of my relationships, including with my mother, would I say that I was "passive." Manipulated and lied to? Oh, yes! But I don't consider myself to be a victim. Accommodating? Yes. I would pick my battles. I was very much an active dance partner and leader with certain controls in my dysfunctional relationships. The key for me was that I was unaware that my subconscious was driving my decisions. Though consciously I wanted a career woman and equal partner who had her stuff together, my subconscious mind wanted a "needy chick" to fix.

What I've learned as I've gained a deeper understanding of myself is that codependents tend to attract people who see themselves as victims. These types of individuals (the "victims") never seem to be able to get their acts together. They wander from one career or job to another. They blame everyone—even the family dog—for why they are unhappy. Their mantra is that if only EVERYONE else would just change their behavior and be nice to them, then they would finally obtain true happiness and enlightenment—nirvana. In reality, even if all of the stars, the sun, and the moon aligned perfectly for them, they would blame planet Earth for not being round enough. Drawn in by their sob song, as if by a snake charmer, codependents believe they are helping their "needy person." More likely, they're tinkering with something that they have no business attempting to fix because they are ill-equipped for what is best addressed by a counselor or psychiatrist. The codependent should just walk away from the "needy person," especially if the person is also an extreme narcissist. Narcissism is not all bad. Most successful people are a bit narcissistic in that they have a high level of confidence. This enables them to achieve and bounce back quickly from losses. However, for example, a person with narcissistic personality disorder is excessively preoccupied with having others praise them, though they have little to no accomplishments to justify it. It's a very complex disorder that is too deep to go into at length here. Basically the person craves constant attention reinforcement in order to avoid feeling the pain that they are causing others in their family or inner circle. Psychologically, they are living in an alternative universe. Visualize, if you will, the sun orchestrating the orbit of the planets and burning them as she pulls them near to her. Where there is a person who has narcissistic personality disorder, you will likely find a codependent who enables her.

The motive behind codependency is almost never sinister, though. You want to be a "do-gooder," but you end up harming yourself, as the person you're trying to help lashes back at you instead. This can particularly be a problem for people who feel strongly that they should be helping their fellow man and woman.

How do you fix someone if they do not perceive themselves to be broken? And is *their* perceived brokenness truly *your* call to make?

Codependents can be very judgmental. In some cases, they enter into a relationship and then determine that their significant other has a weakness. Meanwhile, the other person's so-called weakness could actually be their key strength. Nonetheless, extreme codependents feel that they have to fix the person and that they are the only one who is up to the task. This stance could also be revealing a certain level of low self-esteem in the codependent. They focus on the other person's perceived problems as a deflection so that they don't have to confront their own issues. They don't want to see their own inadequacies, so they make themselves feel better by focusing on the inadequacies (or perceived inadequacies) of someone else.

Was the Wallerstein and Lewis study 100 percent spot-on in describing my codependency? No, but I definitely saw a lot of myself in that study. Do you see *yourself* in any of this? If so, it's time to start dealing with it.

TRUST VERSUS MISTRUST

Everybody has a trust issue. The old "nature vs. nurture" discussion clearly indicates that how we come to perceive ourselves is a combination of our genetics and our environmental exposure. We are born with personality traits, but our environmental influences and how we respond to them also shape who we are. When it comes to trust, much of this can be traced to attachment style, which can refer to how you display affection toward another person. This often stems from your experience as a baby and then continues throughout your life as people show themselves to be trustworthy or not.

Trust is a healthy bond where you feel that you can rely on someone or something to be there for you. You feel a sense of safety and security. Let's start with "attachment theory" to get a better grasp of all this. Basically, this theory says that to obtain successful emotional development, an infant needs a healthy bond with at least one primary caregiver. The caregiver can be male or female. Developmental psychologist Mary Ainsworth in the 1960s and 1970s did what is referred to as the Strange Situation Protocol, where she found different patterns of attachment in children depending on their early caregiving environments. The patterns helped shape expectations, or levels of trust, later in life.

In the experiment, the infants' interest level to explore activities with a researcher was observed when the infants' caregivers were present and then removed for a significant length of time. The four attachment classifications are secure attachment, anxious-ambivalent attachment, anxious-avoidant attachment, and disorganized attachment.

Infants with a secure attachment style were initially upset when the caregiver left, but eventually bonded with the researcher and explored the room. This was because their caregiver was often very attentive to them when they were present. The anxious-ambivalent attachment style infant typically didn't explore much. They were stressed by strangers when the caregiver was present and even more so when the caregiver was away. This happened, in part, as a reaction to the caregiver's unpredictable behavior.

The anxious-avoidant infant didn't react much to the caregiver when they were present *or* away. Measurements showing a high heart rate response indicated that the infant was masking stress. After reaching out to their caregivers and being rejected often, these infants developed an "I don't care" persona. The child learned how to control the pain of rejection, but the pain was still there. The disorganized/disoriented attachment style refers to a variety of complex responses from the infant that can combine some of the other attachment styles. It can range from fear, to jerking back and forth, to disassociating with the caregiver. These infants were often linked with caregivers who had experienced major traumas and who were themselves depressed.

What does this have to do with marriage relationships? Well, several studies, such as by the National Institute of Child Health and Human Development, indicate a connection between early childhood experiences and the adults we become. If you learn as an infant not to trust your caregiver, then chances are you won't develop a trusting relationship with that "best friend" in kindergarten. If as you move through your K-12 years and your parents or caregivers continue to be untrustworthy, it could shape your relationships with your peers when you're a teen. If your childhood was filled with distrustful relationships, why would you miraculously become a married adult who trusts their spouse completely and unconditionally?

LOVE IS PAIN?

As in the case with how our attachment styles develop, our understanding of love is rooted in nature and nurture. Sadly, many people believe that love is supposed to be painful because of the relationship models to which they have been exposed. They have been conditioned to believe that unless the person they are in a relationship with is causing them physical or mental anguish, they are not truly in love. But I'm here to tell you, that's not love. Love is defined as "a profoundly tender, passionate affection for another person." The word tender means "soft or delicate in substance." The word affection means "a gentle feeling of fondness or liking." Passion? Yes, but there's nothing in the definition that says be aggressive, angry, yell, scream, and hit, or be a manipulative abuser. To do any of these things obviously contradicts the definition of love. Based on this, I say that a person who believes love MUST be painful has a warped mindset. I call it "functional insanity."

A lot of people have mental disorders but are able to function—like the neighborhood alcoholic who acts like a wild man the previous evening, but gets up the next morning and puts on his uniform and goes to work on time. If while you are dating you now find yourself behaving like this regarding love, certainly this will be a major problem later if you marry. If you believe that marrying the person and having children will solve the problem, then you are among the ranks of the many that tragically enter marriage in this way.

On my radio show, relationship expert and life coach Tony Gaskins Jr. shared his story about the personal impact of being raised in an argument-fueled environment. Gaskins has helped several people ranging from every day folks to celebrities get their relationships on track. In sharing his personal testimony on radio, Gaskins said that he grew up watching conflicts among his parents, married relatives, and others in the neighborhood and naturally figured that arguments and conflicts were normal. So when he got married, he followed suit. Additionally, Gaskins said he was a womanizer, liar and cheater because he saw that behavior modeled as a child. His rascal ways went on for the first two years of his marriage. However, his wife put a stop to it by leaving him. She had seen her mother put an end to the madness during her own marriage by leaving her father, Gaskins said. His wife clearly had a different model, so therefore, she had a different image of what a marriage rooted in love should look like. This triggered in Gaskins the realization that his wife was a jewel who respected herself, and that he could not afford to let her go. "It's usually one party that appreciates the chaos and control and keeps their partner in the dark and it gives them control," Gaskins said. "People act out of their learned behaviors."

After his wife left him, Gaskins made a vow to himself and to his wife that he would turn his behavior around and become a good husband, and in doing so, he got his wife back. During the radio interview, Gaskins said that it had been about five years since he and his wife (to whom he had been married seven years at the time of this writing) had a blowout argument or got angry at each other to the point of ignoring one another. If they have a disagreement now, he said, they talk about it from the heart, rather than getting wrapped up in emotions.

In recent years, Gaskins has obviously done a good job cleaning the dirty laundry that was in his luggage and re-stuffing it with fresh shirts and pants, but for many of those who haven't arrived at this point in their journey of self-discovery, they can't imagine being in a relationship without cheating and lying, fussing and fighting. That, Gaskins said, is because they haven't seen relationships other than those kinds. If things are peaceful and the person who believes love equals pain is not used to that, they will get antsy. To get things back to their idea of *normal*, they will engage in disruptive behavior by pushing emotional buttons. The partner who prefers peace will begin to accommodate their chaotic mate. They'll make excuses for them that eventually lead to slipping into the darkness of chaos. It's not always a case of the one who likes the chaos being the aggressor. For example, a person who is normally laidback and calm could become the aggressor. This happens because in their desire to meet the needs of their marriage prospect or spouse, they take on the behavior patterns that the other person craves. In an odd way, the other person prefers being abused because it is a more familiar situation to them. It is their comfort zone.

Can you see yourself not becoming enraged with your spouse, but instead always resolving disagreements peacefully and respectfully? Personally, I believe that married couples *can* always resolve their disagreements respectfully, but I did not always see it this way. Because of my upbringing and the influences of pop culture's image of marriage, I bought into the warped belief that yelling and screaming hurtful words is just part of being married. I see now that this is a result of the mistake of trying to "make it work" instead of "letting it work." If you truly care for someone and you've been honest about dealing with your own luggage, you will strive to NOT wound your current or future spouse, including with words.

GETTING HELP

Whether it is codependency or trust issues, or the warped idea that love is pain, the good news is that you can get the help necessary to change. Even though these syndromes or conditions are rooted in your childhood, it's never too late to improve as an adult. Like erasing unnecessary files on your computer, you can always reformat your mental hard drive. Again, I am a strong proponent of getting good professional counseling. It has helped me. There's no shame in it. There's no shame in having a mental health disorder either. Counseling can help you process the information in your head and give you the tools to sort things out.

Pam Bell, a Baltimore-area-based counselor (she's also my sister that I was raised with) who also appeared on my radio show, takes her engaged clients through a 12-step premarital session. One of the key sessions is on knowing yourself first. She takes her clients through assessment tests such as Myers-Briggs, which measures psychological preferences. Another type of test is the DiSC Assessment, which is a personality profile. What these types of assessments do is help you to see your tendencies in terms of how you perceive the world. You also get to see how your marriage prospect sees the world and what you both need to do to coexist. Knowing yourself first is about helping you to hone in on your areas of strength and weakness so that you can grow toward being the best you can be.

Reading academic research studies by mental health experts and spiritual and self-help books—as well as listening to and/or watching inspirational recordings—can also help you to reformat or reboot your love life. After a painful relationship, a good friend of mine reformatted his mental hard drive by listening to inspirational tapes from life coaches, such as Gaskins. He would listen to the audio every morning while driving to and from work. Eventually, he began to think differently and to behave differently as he followed the instructions offered by the coach. The results eventually yielded him the results he sought—a beautiful, intelligent and kind wife who would give birth to their two children.

Make the mature decision to reformat your mental hard drive, like Gaskins did his. Make the best decision you can at the moment of which you have the most control—now. The following are some resources that can help you do that and to get to know yourself:

Psychology and Personality Resources

- National Institute of Child Health indicate: https://www.nichd.nih.gov/publications/pubs/documents/seccyd_06.pdf

- Center for Disease Control (Childhood Development): http://www.cdc.gov/ncbddd/childdevelopment/

- Psychology Today: http://www.psychologytoday.com/

- Myers-Briggs Type Indicator: http://www.myersbriggs.org/

- DiSC Profile: www.discprofile.com

Life Coaching and Counseling

- Pam Bell: www.serenitypcc.com

- Tony Gaskins Jr.: www.tonygaskins.com

- Life Coaching for Personal and Professional Empowerment: www.lifecoaching.com

- International Coaching Federation: http://www.coachfederation.org/

- Life Coach.com: www.lifecoach.com

- American Counseling Association: www.counseling.org

- Mayo Clinic Premarital Counseling: http://www.mayoclinic.org/tests-procedures/premarital-counseling/basics/definition/prc-20013242

MY STORY: RESOLVING MY CODEPENDENCY

After I realized I was a codependent and began to better understand how my own family history had affected my role in love relationships and marriage, I began talking to my mother about our common past. We talked honestly and openly about many issues. We discussed the things that I didn't like. We talked about her divorce from my father and how I was affected. There were no secrets or animosities left on the table. We unpacked our luggage and cleaned our laundry together. I told her often that I loved her, and she knew it. She told me often that she loved me, and I knew it. I came to a point of peace where I accepted and loved her for who she was, but also where I would love her on terms that worked best for me. I am so thankful that I accomplished this with her. A few years after this talk, my mother developed Alzheimer's, and those deep conversations we had where she would share her wisdom (including spot-on truths regarding my *so-called marriage*) came to a sudden end.

Eventually my mom no longer recognized her youngest son. That too was a very dark day for me. Still, I was thankful that my mother was alive and that I could visit with her. On December 29, 2012, Eudora E. LaVeist transitioned to a much happier home. I think about her every day.

RECAP

As I said, take it from me: You've got to take responsibility for getting yourself "right" before you get married. Unpack those major unresolved hurts, insecurities, pet peeves, bad habits, and the like that you've been dragging around throughout your life. Are you a codependent like I was? Do you have trust issues? Do you mistakenly think that you can't have love unless you are also in pain? Do the work that's necessary to reformat your mental hard drive before you try to link and sync up with someone else. Get individual counseling and work with a life coach. Read scriptures, and inspirational and academic books on the topics that you are struggling with. Apply the solutions offered that relate to you. If you don't take these steps first, you will potentially just bring misery to the other person, which, in turn, will bring more pain to yourself—unless of course, you like being in pain.

CHAPTER 2

WARNING SIGNS: YOU GET WHAT YOU SEE

Dear Daughter,

One day, I had lunch with a former student at one of the local colleges where I teach. A funny thing is that she knows you. Anyway, the conversation went from her career—she's now a successful media professional—to her family, to her relationship with her boyfriend of a few years. She shared that she was getting tired of the guy being a little possessive and clingy. He was her college sweetheart, but she was maturing as a professional woman and her interests and tastes were evolving. She was thinking of ending the relationship. I told her that with her media career on the rise, she likely needed to be with someone who wasn't insecure with her success and who would not feel threatened by other men, particularly when the two of them were at public functions together. "If you're the emcee of a gala and you're working the room and mingling with guests, you don't need a guy who will be at the table alone pouting because you're not there holding his hand," I said.

She agreed, and we left the conversation at that. But then about one month later, I ran into her at an event and noticed something glistening on her finger.

"Is this what it looks like?" I asked as I pointed at her left hand.

"Yeah, it is," she responded with a shy grin.

"The same guy you were talking about dumping that day at lunch?" I asked.

"Yeah, it is," she said.

"But —"

"Weeeelllll," she interrupted. "I felt that he needed to take me a little more seriously, so I decided to back off and create some distance between us. He got the message that if he didn't get his act together that he could lose me. So he got his act together, I guess."

Our conversation was cut short as people who knew us came by to say hello. She got pulled away. I had some important marriage advice for her, but we never finished the conversation. I wanted to warn her that she had likely planted a seed for a future divorce.

Most divorces begin happening BEFORE the marriage. Instead of being honest about the warning signs that the person is not "the right one," many of us plow ahead believing grass and flowers will grow over the problems. Eventually those same warning signs that were seen, but glossed over turn into weeds that choke out of its misery a marriage that either should have been suffocated before it began or should have undergone substantial triage in the form of premarital counseling to get the couple in sync.

What are warning signs? They are issues that can range from differences of opinion on politics and race, to whether someone smokes, to how you feel about tattoos. A warning sign can be an issue that, like in the example of my former student's fiancé, the person is insecure.

If you are human, you have flaws. If you are human, you are going to make mistakes. If you are human, you are going to disappoint your partner. No matter how frivolous someone else outside the relationship may think your issue with your marriage prospect is, whatever truly matters to you and your partner could become a deal breaker. It is vital to be honest about the warning signs that are showing you the deal should not be entered into, the contract left unsigned. It is vital that you address the signs openly and honestly to get a clear understanding of how you are both going to deal with them (or not deal with them) going forward. Daughter, you've heard me say this many times, but I'll repeat it: If the person you are dating has a behavior pattern or habit that rubs you the wrong way, ask yourself, "If this thing that bothers me about this person never changes, could I live with it?" If your answer is no, then it is best that you what? Right, end the dating relationship now. Just be friends. Don't fool yourself into thinking that YOU will somehow change him, or influence him to change. You have no right to force a person to meet your expectations. Individual change is up to HIM to make, not YOU. Deal-breakers are called "deal-breakers" because they are deal-breakers! Remember, when you are not honest about the deal-breakers before saying "I do," you are basically tilling the soil for when you will eventually say "I don't" want to be married to this person anymore. Trust me, Daughter. That is not a good feeling.

This chapter will provide you with clues that will help you spot warning signs. Again, don't ignore them or think they'll disappear after you marry. They are symptoms of larger problems that will only get worse. The fact is, what you "get" in someone is what you "see." I know that the saying is typically written, "What you see is what you get." Like "It's Cheaper to Keep Her," this saying was actually a popular song, too. But I stress that what you GET *is* what you SEE because we have a tendency to disbelieve and ignore our eyes and our gut. Despite what we clearly see, we keep telling ourselves that we are going to get a different result later. No. Keep your eyes open and see your boyfriend or girlfriend for who they really are NOW, not who you wish them to be. Doing so can make all the difference in the world between being a happily married man or woman versus becoming part of the growing statistic of the majority of divorced Americans.

Let's take a look at the type of signs that should make you run and never turn back.

WARNING SIGNS
NUMBERS DON'T LIE

Numbers can be great storytellers. Rarely do they lie. You can tell a lot about a person by looking at the numbers associated with them in two very personal areas: their cell phone bill and their bank and/or tax statements. If you're dating someone, it will likely be hard for you to get access to their bank account or tax statements (unless you're living with them, which I do not recommend at all as a marriage test drive—I'll go into more detail about this later). So I'm actually not going to say much about the statements, other than what my tax accountant loves to tell me: "Dude, you eat out at restaurants too much." But on cell phones, I have much to say. If you're dating, it is possible that you will be able to access your marriage prospect's cell phone bill . . . and learn a lot about him or her. In fact, a lot of dating couples share cell phone plans, a notion that makes me scratch my head, but keep following me . . .

The information the cell phone bill reveals is priceless. The numbers that a person calls and/or texts most represent what or who he or she is most involved in, whether it's regarding their work or personal life. For example, let's say that as you look at a phone bill and peer down the listing of numbers, you see a particular number that is being called or texted often. Down the list, line by line turns into a cluster of the same phone number. The calls or texts to this number are made around the same time early in the morning (say before 7 a.m.) when your marriage prospect should be waking, or after midnight, when they should be asleep. There's a story there. Calls of 30 minutes or an hour or longer represent a significant conversation, obviously. Several texts back and forth with the same number mean a conversation was going on. Pay very, very close attention: Has this been a consistent pattern for some time? Your marriage prospect may not be having virtual prayer meetings every morning and evening. They are likely cheating.

A scenario similar to this actually happened to the daughter of another guest on my radio show. After the on-air interview, the guest and I began chatting about other things. This is typical after an interview as guests become more comfortable after we've been talking and bonding while on air. We began chatting about our college-age adult children. The guest said that her daughter decided to put her boyfriend, who was away at college, on her cell phone plan to help him out. His phone had been cut off because of non-payment. Of course, she wanted to be able to talk to him regularly. Besides, they were planning to get married after they both graduated from college.

The first few months, things were fine. But then the phone bill under the boyfriend's number began coming in higher and higher. The daughter was not able to actually see the contents of her boyfriend's text messages, but she could see the numbers that he texted or called. She began seeing a particular number show up regularly. My guest said that she tried to explain to her daughter what was really happening, but her daughter didn't want to hear it.

Because of privacy reasons, you would have to get a court order to see the actual text messages, such as, "GM luva. U wer gr8! LN … Kaboom! LOL. :-)." There are apps that can allow you to see the texts, though, if that's what you truly want to spend your energy doing. If you've got to go that far, it's probably clear that you've got a deal-breaker on your hands. As a journalist, and, as I write this, a doctoral candidate in technology and media studies, I know how to do computer-assisted investigative reporting, and I know research methods. Private investigators, lawyers, marketers, data miners, journalists—we're all cousins when it comes to analyzing information about human behavior. But it doesn't take a computer scientist to figure out this cell phone caper.

Just use your good old common sense! Why else would someone consistently text a "friend" *that* early in the morning or late at night? Even if you're not married, but dating or engaged, and you live apart (or are away at college), shouldn't it be YOU that they're texting at those times? Why would there be lengthy phone calls or several clusters of texts to the same number during lunch breaks or the afternoon commute home? The story is that your marriage prospect (in this case, the daughter's boyfriend) is *sexting*. Those photos they texted were likely selfies—pictures of themselves standing in the bathroom bearing a naked chest. Or perhaps photos of their body jewelry attached to their very private space below their waist.

Hey! Not just high school and college kids, but middle-aged adults also flirt on social media websites. Trying to recapture some past glory that likely never was, these middle-aged kids keep photos of themselves in their smartphones and share them too. This is the modern digital world of premarital and marriage relationships. It is what it is. The quote, "Common sense is not common," is credited to Voltaire, the famous French philosopher and writer of the Enlightenment period. There obviously were no mobile phones back in the 1700s, but certainly men and women were cheating. Cheating is a clear sign that something deeper is wrong with the relationship. People will lie, but cell phone numbers can't. Those numbers have a story to tell that you would be foolish to ignore.

SEX

All this talk about sexting leads to the obvious and perhaps ultimate deal breaker—sex. If two people have very different expectations and/or needs concerning sex, this can lead to cheating down the road and/or extreme frustration and ultimately a marriage that dies. What are your thoughts regarding sex in the marriage? Do you feel that you would want to have sex with your spouse every day or two or three times per week? Do you consider yourself to have a high libido or low? Do you even think sex is necessary to have intimacy? Do you believe intimacy is important? These questions, especially the last one, may seem obvious, but they are not. Everyone does not view sex or intimacy in the same way. Some people are uncomfortable talking about sex, or, as is the case with some heterosexual couples, don't see it as important to the marriage other than to have children. What is important is that both spouses share compatible views concerning sex. For example, if both partners do not feel that having sex regularly is important, then they are as compatible as partners who agree that they ought to have sex every day (good luck with sustaining that).

Another important issue: Both partners should be clear about their lovemaking preferences. One way to slay a marriage is for a partner to start off having sex in a manner that their mate enjoys, only to one day abruptly withhold having sex in that way. A close friend of mine gave me permission to tell this very personal story. As part of his and his wife's lovemaking, they engaged in a specific sexual practice for several years into the marriage. Then one day, she stopped engaging in that practice with him. He did not pay it much attention, though. The next few times they made love, he noticed it again. He finally asked her why. She told him that sometime previously while she was performing the act, he touched her in a manner that reminded her of a bad sexual experience she had had when she was a teen (the couple are in their late 30s). So a trauma that had happened more than 15 years ago, that had nothing to do with her husband, was suddenly now impacting their marriage intimacy. At the time, my friend had no clue that he had touched his wife in a manner that triggered her memory of the past trauma. Nonetheless, he couldn't handle this sudden "change in the action." He soon went outside of the marriage to have his perceived need fulfilled. Not engaging in this specific sexual practice with his wife was apparently a deal-breaker for him.

To some couples this may seem like a silly, shallow dispute. Other people have open marriages, where sex with others is permissible. Again, the key theme you should have picked up in this book by now is that couples should determine for themselves what works best for them. Heck, you both may even decide that you don't really need intercourse to make love! You express your love for each other in other ways. Personally, I believe that lovemaking should be a celebration of the deeper "between the ears" relationship that the couple enjoys outside of the bed. The physical intimacy is an extension of the love, friendship and commitment they share even if they can no longer physically perform sexual intercourse.

To me, this situation with my friend is less about sex than it is about trust and empathy—trust yourself and each other enough to be honest; before you act, think of the impact of your actions on the other person. Perhaps had my friend and his wife focused more on developing their sexual relationship from the neckline up, this would not have become an issue or it could have been resolved. The wife would have been better able to unpack her luggage first and not allow the trauma that she can't undo to enter their marriage bed. She essentially brought another man into their bedroom by way of her mind. The wife also would have been able to talk honestly with her husband about the problem and they could have both sought a solution together—even professionally. Apparently, the husband hadn't reassured his bride that she could trust him to understand her feelings. My friend could have been more understanding of his wife's unresolved issues, and should not have sought to have his merely physical (or was it *just* physical?) need met elsewhere.

WORKING AND MONEY EXPECTATIONS

Do you believe that both spouses should work, or that it's OK to live off one income? Do you believe that you should pay your bills together, or should you split the bills and pay them separately? Should you have a joint account or separate accounts? Should your paychecks be deposited directly into your accounts, or are you the type of person who still likes to walk up to the teller, cash your check, and feel your money in your hands? I can go on, but these are all crucial issues that should be clearly addressed before getting married. If you and your partner are on completely different pages on these issues, all the money in the world won't prevent you from avoiding severe problems in your marriage.

Money and working are so important to the success of a marriage that the topic receives elaborate treatment in Chapter 4, "It's NOT Always Cheaper to Keep Her (or Him)."

WHAT BUGS THEM

If your significant other flies off the handle over small things, how will he or she react to the big issues? Keep this question in mind as you discover their triggers. Sometimes you can find the clues in the most mundane scenarios and places.

Consider this "car" story that involves a man at the wheel, his girlfriend as the co-pilot, and her chatty sister as the backseat driver. The three were driving to a family gathering in another state. The man insisted that he knew where he was going and didn't need the GPS.

"You all rely too much on technology," he said. "Back in the day, people traveled according to the position of the sun and the moon."

As they drove along the highway, the sister kept reminding the guy that his exit was coming up.

"I've got this," he'd say with a slight attitude.

As they continued to drive, what should have been a one-hour and 15-minute trip began approaching two hours.

"Honey, are we almost there?" his girlfriend asked.

"Yeah, I've got this," he said with a slight attitude again.

"We were supposed to be there about 30 minutes ago. Are you sure?" she responded.

"I've got this, I've got this," he repeated with a more emphasized attitude.

"Yeah, you got this alright. You got this trip turned into a journey to no time soon," the chatty sister said. "You're just like my ex-husband, Wilbert. Don't want to follow directions. Don't want to admit when you're wrong."

"Yeah, I think it's obvious why he's your ex-husband," the boyfriend responded.

"Honey, didn't you say something about getting off at Exit

50?" his girlfriend asked. "Aren't we coming up on Exit 150?"

"Why don't you both stop nagging," he yelled. "I told you I've got this!"

They were indeed going the wrong way and were one hour and 30 minutes off course.

"Honey, why can't you just listen?" his girlfriend said. "We need to turn around."

His pride kept him driving off course for another 30 minutes.

If a person gets bent out of shape over small things, you can bet they will trip over big things. Potential deal breaker. Don't ignore it.

WHAT'S IN THEIR HOME

Another great place to pick up premarital data is by visiting a person's home. The pictures and paintings on their walls tell something about what they value (family, friends) and their overall taste, and whether their kitchen seems to be used regularly and its level of cleanliness tells a story about their eating habits. Is their home cluttered? This is a likely indication that their thoughts may be disorderly, too. Cluttered may actually work for you. You might like living that way, or you might be the one to bring the sense of order that the person has been wanting for their own life. The point is to be observant and to think seriously about whether the person's current living condition is something you can deal with long-term. Certainly, during the dating phase, people put on their best appearance, but there are a few key places in the home that tell the true tale of how the person is living—their bedroom closet, their personal bathroom, and under their bed.

I once visited the home of a woman I was dating and put to work my attention to detail. The living room area was very neat. The rug was vacuumed. The kitchen was cleaned. I asked to use her bathroom. It was also in decent shape. After drying my hands, I took a peek into her walk-in closet, which was just to my left. What did I see? Clothes on the floor and shoes on top of them. Her idea of cleaning up was to basically throw everything into the closet. I bent down and looked under her bed, which was neatly made. Too bad underneath was a different story—

dinner plates and cups, shoes, underwear, and a potato chips bag. The lady was very attractive and dressed very nice, but she was an undercover slob. Her idea of "cleaning up" was to cover up. Potential deal breaker. (Yes, I snooped, but I had been invited into her home to get to know her more, so I felt my poking around was within limits.)

Being too neat can be problematic, too. A lady friend told me that she visited the apartment of a man that she was very interested in for a Saturday brunch. Inside it was immaculate, which initially impressed her. He poured her a glass of cranberry juice and they sipped, ate fruits he had prepared—kiwi, pineapples and pears—and chatted. As they talked and ate, her glass was about 10 percent empty. She decided to go to the bathroom. Inside along the double sink were peach- and green-coded toothpicks stacked neatly side by side. They matched the walls, which were peach with green trim. The toilet seat was violet, as well as the mats. The bathroom was so equally immaculate that she was afraid that tinkling might mess it up. She decided to just hold it until she left. She washed her hands. When she returned to the dining area, she noticed that he had already poured out her glass of cranberry juice and washed it. He wore peach-colored rubber gloves. She paused and looked at him, puzzled.

"What?" he said.

Being clean, like in the military, is fine, but this guy is a little too exxxxtra, she thought to herself. She couldn't visualize living with someone who has obsessive-compulsive disorder.

"Oh, nothing," she responded.

Deal breaker.

POLITICS

Are you a Republican or a member of the Democratic Party (or as Republicans like to quip, 'Democrat Party')? Are you an Independent, like I am? Heck, are you a member of the Tea Party or Green Party? Are you a conservative or progressive? Your politics can have a major impact on your ability to have a healthy marriage. If you're not talking about children or work, there's a good chance that you'll be talking about politics or the next "hot rail" topic below, religion. Politics is one of those hot-button issues that people lose their minds over.

In America and across the world, as ideological movements grip crowds of people, we seem to be in an era where we are becoming more and more defined by what we say we believe. People are even beginning to cross traditional racial and ethnic lines to unite around a cause that is typically one or two narrow issues. We have also become more polarized. Politicians pounce on this for personal gain. I covered the historic 2008 presidential victory of President Barack Obama. While on the field among the news media when Obama accepted the Democratic nomination, I witnessed the euphoria among the rainbow of faces in the stadium in Denver. The historic presidential election of 2016 where Republican Donald Trump shockingly defeated Democrat Hillary Clinton has re-exposed how at odds Americans have remained for generations. The U.S. Congress has not gotten much bipartisan legislation passed because legislators on both sides are focused more on pandering to the narrow issues of the voters in their individual districts. They fear being booted out of their jobs. This reality is playing out in the homes of voters, many of whom are married. If you and your marriage prospect are on polar opposite sides of important issues, you can count on this exploding in your home at the dinner table or in the bedroom.

People of very different political views have had successful marriages. The key is to have ground rules of engagement that you both agree on. Work these out beforehand. If you can't work these out, it would be foolish to plow through with the marriage, thinking that things will miraculously get better somehow.

Another issue is marrying someone who has no interest in politics at all. Let me share with you the story of a political science professor I know, a woman who lives and breathes politics. She once directed communications for a major political party. However, her spouse had no interest in politics. In fact, he expressed a hate for it. What message do you think that sent to his political junkie wife? What a person does for a career can be an inseparable element of their identity. If you hate what a person does, especially if the person is passionate about it and thus spends significant hours doing it, then what true feelings might you also be revealing about the person you claim to love? Think about it. This makes as much sense as telling your children, "I hate your no good deadbeat father." What message are you ultimately delivering to your children about your feelings towards them?

RELIGION

There is a Bible Scripture, 2 Corinthians 6:14, that reads: "Be ye not unequally yoked together with unbelievers: For what fellowship hath righteousness with unrighteousness? And what communion hath light with darkness?" The "unequally yoked" imagery here is of two horses pulling a chariot or carriage that are yoked or harnessed together. If the harness isn't balanced, they'll pull against each other, which would be very bad for the person sitting in the carriage. There are a lot of interpretations (and misinterpretations) of what this Scripture is saying. Some believe it means that Christians should only marry other Christians. Some have misapplied it believing that if you are having trouble communicating with and being understood by your mate, then you are probably unequally yoked. Basically, the Scripture is warning that a believer in God should not marry a person who rejects God (unbelievers).

The simple truth is that there are many successful marriages in which people practice different religions, and obviously many unsuccessful marriages of people practicing the same faith. The key to success is understanding your differences, whether you are a believer, agnostic or atheist, while being true to yourselves and focusing on your commonalities. If you can't come to this understanding beforehand, do not go to the altar.

If you both find that you understand and can respect each other despite your different faiths or lack of faith, there is still a critical question you must answer before moving forward with marriage: You should both decide if you're in agreement on how you'll raise your children—whose faith will they be raised under, or will they be given the option to choose their belief system or religion? Will they experience both faiths equally? People all over are making this work by communicating openly and honestly. If you're at a loggerheads over this, and you indeed want children, then you've got a problem. If you can't come to a resolution, don't marry.

CHILDREN

While growing up, my daughter would often say that she wants at least six children after she marries. Rather than be discouraging, I would just laugh, shake my head and say, "Well, I guess you are going to be very successful and rich in your profession. I hope you remember me when I'm old and can't go to the bathroom without help."

"TMI., Dad, TMI," she typically says, short speak for "too much information."

If my daughter remains serious about this six children thing, I strongly suggest that she and her marriage prospect get on the same page about it.

The fact is, you and your potential spouse must agree on whether you want children, and if you do, how many and how you would raise them. This is serious. If you disagree on even one of these points, DON'T GET MARRIED.

In 2017, the U.S. Department of Agriculture released its annual "Cost of Raising a Child" estimates that in America it costs $233.610 to raise a child to age 18. Take it from me: Not only is rearing children extremely expensive, but if you take parenting seriously, it will be one of the most difficult things you'll ever do! If you don't want children, but jump into a marriage with someone who does, you will potentially be hurting at least one other person: the eventual child who results. By law, your lack of desire for having children won't let you off the hook when it comes to their care and simply doing right by them. So if you and your partner can't agree on the "child" question, get off this road now, because there are no U-turns.

INTERRACIAL MARRIAGE

Interracial marriages have become more acceptable in America. In 2010, they hit a high of 8.4 percent compared to 3 percent in 1980, according to a Pew Research Center study. Of the 275,500 interracial marriages in 2010, 43 percent were White/Hispanic, 14.4 percent were White/Asian, and 11.9 percent were White/Black. Gallup's 2013 Minority Rights and Relations poll of 4,373 Americans, including 1,010 non-Hispanic

Blacks, revealed that 87 percent of Americans approve of Black/White marriage compared to 4 percent in 1958. Blacks approve of marriages to Whites at 96 percent, while the White approval rate is 84 percent.

Many people are themselves products of interracial marriages and then enter into interracial marriages that are of a different racial combination! Clearly, interracial marriages are more acceptable, which is great. However, challenges remain for those who are in such relationships. Therefore, interracial couples should consider pausing to discuss the issues they are likely to confront.

Talks with people who are in interracial marriages have revealed that one of the biggest challenges they face is the perception that if a person is in a relationship with someone outside of their race, they *must* be rejecting their own race. All racial and ethnic groups in America have been subjected to negative stereotypes. If you feel that you couldn't deal with family members' or friends' harsh judgment of you because of the race of the mate you choose, you'd better think seriously about your fortitude in going forward with the marriage. If others' views mean that much to you, then your own feelings for your potential spouse may not be strong enough to help a marriage between the two of you survive.

A few other considerations:

How does your marriage prospect talk about people of your race in general? Do they buy into the negative stereotypes of your race, even though they seem to not impose those stereotypes on you? Do they instead put you on a pedestal? Do they say things like, "You're not like the rest of them. You're different." This could be a sign that the person is only involved with you because they are looking for *the experience* of being with someone of a different race. In other words, they may be wanting to check off the exotic sexual experience box from their bucket list.

How would you raise your biological interracial children? You must absolutely get on the same page regarding how you would raise your children to identify racially. Do you want them to identify by your race, but your future spouse thinks they should identify by his or her race or as mixed race? If you and your partner can't agree on these questions, don't bring a child into the world to muddle through the confusion you will create.

What consenting people do in any type of legal marriage is their business. Square away the issues before you make your commitment legal. You should be on the same page about children, work, money, and many other fundamentals. If you're not, and you try but can't get there, don't tie the knot because it will become a noose.

IT'S ALL IN THE PSYCHOLOGY

Citing Erik Erikson's theory of psychosocial development, psychologists will tell you that certain aspects of an individual's personality develop over different life stages. Each stage builds on the previous. If a person failed to develop a healthy sense of trust in their infant stage (remember attachment styles?), they'll likely struggle with trust issues during the adolescent stage when they should be developing a healthy sense of identity. Of course, when you're initially attracted to someone because of their long hair, six-pack abs, or sexy smile, you have no idea what's been going on between their ears. The young adult stage is roughly from 19 to 40, which is also when the need to develop intimate relationships is highest. These are the prime marriage years. It's also one of the longest development stages, which means personalities don't change much unless there is a major traumatic event that turns into a crossroads. For example, the death of a loved one could cause you to think more deeply about your own life and the need to make major changes. Or losing all of your wealth can dramatically change your perspective on life and how you treat people.

If you're in your 30s or 40s, think about some of the people you knew back in your 20s. Have they really changed much? Sure, they've likely put on more pounds, or they've read a few more books, or taken some overseas trips and cruises. They may have evolved in their careers or made a lot of money, which has changed their social status. But have they REALLY changed personality-wise? The same people who relied on their family name to obtain social status on campus are still relying on their family name. The military buddy who was always boasting about all the A-list Hollywood actors he hung out with when he was back home in Arkansas is still lying. Your patient engineer husband is now basically the same patient, sweet engineering major that he was in college. And if you are the college-educated clingy wife who feels threatened by the checkout girl at the 7-Eleven who smiles at your husband while handing over your change, your husband should recall that you acted the same way in college when you were his girlfriend. Unless you've "womaned up" and have confronted your issues head on, you remain the same low self-esteem girl who was threatened by the sorority sisters who flirted with your then boyfriend at the fraternity party.

RECAP

People do not and will not change, unless they decide for themselves to reformat their mental hard drives. Why am I telling you all this? Because it bears repeating: If someone is exhibiting a warning sign that spells "deal breaker," you need to take it seriously. Chances are, what you're seeing in them is what you'll get from them for the rest of your life. That's not always the case, but like I said earlier, if someone changes, it usually happens when they are jolted into a major crossroads that causes them to deeply evaluate themselves and their choices and to reprogram their thinking. This is not something that YOU can force upon the person you're considering marrying any more than they can force it upon you.

Whether a person decides to change their flaws is between them and the universe. When you see a flaw that is a potential deal breaker, you can and should voice your concern to your partner in love, but that's about it. The same rule applies to them. Rather than focus on another person's flaws, focus on fixing your own, as we discussed in Chapter 1. Focus on your development in the life stage that you are in. To go into a marriage expecting you can change someone is a setup for a long slog filled with unrealistic expectations and disappointments. You will only become frustrated, and you will likely find yourself making bad decisions to self-medicate (cheating on your mate, using drugs, gambling, overeating, just to name a few things), which will poison the marriage more.

People can convince themselves to do anything, given

enough time for frustration to boil into justification. The best way to handle a marriage deal breaker is to not deal with it at all. Take off the blinders and get to stepping NOW before the two hearts go shopping for that diamond and/or gold band. Fold your cards and walk away from the game table.

CHAPTER 3
PREMARITAL COUNSELING

Dear Daughter,

The pain that both of us have had to endure has been horrific. It's even worse for you because there is so much more that you want to find out and need to know. But know that like recovering from major surgery, the scars might remain, but healing will continue. Why? Because of our faith in God, our faith in each other, your faith in yourself and the help we've received, including professional counseling. One of the silver linings in all of this is that we have both gained a deeper appreciation of quality professional counseling. A lot of people resist professional counseling because of pride and ignorance. They say things like, "I don't need anybody all up in my business." Even if they give in and go for a session (one or two sessions is not nearly enough), they often quit, claiming, "It just wasn't for me." The truth is that anyone who has experienced a major trauma in their life like we have needs help to process it and heal so that they can move on successfully.

As I have said many times, dealing with your individual baggage is vital. However, before two individuals become one, they should sit together with a marriage counselor. The sessions will help them to see whether the union is likely to work. After all, even two healthy individuals can make an unhealthy marriage!

I should have had premarital counseling. Close family members, like your Aunt Pam, and friends know that several counseling sessions occurred over the years because I was in a "make it work" mode. In hindsight, this was a clear sign of a bad fit. (There also was joint counseling during the months prior to the divorce—too late!) I'm certain that premarital counseling would have given me a better understanding of what I was actually getting myself into. Counseling could have unearthed the hidden agendas and deal-breaking issues, including my own that I was unaware of and or ignoring. Like most couples, I was primarily operating based on what I saw growing up in my childhood home, neighborhood and on TV. As you know, both sets of your grandparents also divorced. Children of divorced parents are more likely to have marriages that end in divorce. Therefore, this includes you. Counseling can help you to evaluate how to take only the best qualities of your parents' marriage and incorporate those into your own. Counseling can help you to learn whether you are truly compatible with the other person. Counseling can help you to decide correctly to NOT go through with it.

OK, so now you've read this book's first two chapters, and you're on your way to getting to know yourself and your potential spouse better, and you've discerned that he comes with no scary warning signs. You've both been working through some of your personal issues, and after all of this, the two of you are convinced that you're made for each other.

I'm glad this book has played a role in getting you to this point, but you still have a bit of work to do before you say your "I do's." If you've come this far in your marriage journey, it's now time to set up a session with a professional counselor.

What You'll Learn from Premarital Counseling

On my radio show, Pam Bell, the counselor I mentioned in Chapter 1, explained that marriage is about two people joining together as one. The saying "opposites attract" is often about two individuals, but the point of the opposites coming together presents an opportunity for the two people to reach new insights to enhance their lives. However, a lot of times people struggle with their differences. For example, one spouse could be cautious when it comes to spending money, while the other is more freewheeling. This can actually be a good counterbalance, encouraging each individual to move out of their comfort zones. When couples resist doing this, they often miss the benefits of growing together in a marriage.

As mentioned previously, Bell takes her clients through a 12-session premarital program. The program represents the 12 months of the year. She begins by exploring what each person believes marriage is about. Is it a contract or a covenant? What should the roles of each person be? She then moves to expectations concerning subjects such as sex, the rearing of children, finances, and the interaction with extended family members and friends. A session on communication is typically a major emphasis. Bell walks couples through the importance of communicating "from the heart," not just from a mental perspective.

"When you speak from the heart and you care for each other, even in the midst of differences, there is a meeting of the hearts," Bell says.

Bell said that people struggle to communicate from the heart effectively because they don't want to submit to each other. Too many people hear the word "submission" and resist as if it is a dirty word. They mistakenly think that to submit is to be subservient or to belittle yourself. There is reason for women in traditional marriages particularly to feel this way because for generations in many cultures, such wives have been treated as property. This still remains the case in certain areas throughout the world, including communities in America. However, submission in the context of marriage means to yield to the other person; the act of yielding is a two-way street. Submission is about both partners being empathetic toward each other. It's about striving to empower each other to achieve the goal of a healthy marriage, from which both partners benefit.

"It takes a stronger person to set aside their beliefs and what they think and to learn, than to stubbornly hold on to your point of view," Bell said. "It's pointless (if your desire is truly to grow) to connect with another person and just want to do things your own way."

In the final premarital sessions, Bell helps couples to develop the tools that will make their marriages last. For example, they explore how couples can create lasting bonds that evolve and strengthen over time.

MOVING FORWARD: SELECTING A COUNSELOR

Premarital counseling is typically performed by licensed therapists who have at minimum graduate degrees in counseling. The fees for the service are often covered by your healthcare insurance plan; however, some counselors do not accept insurance and charge clients per session in the same way that a hairstylist or barber will charge for a haircut.

When choosing your counselor, inquire about their credentials, years of experience, and any other concerns that you may have. Interview them as if you are considering hiring them for a high-level position at your company. In fact, you actually are! At this point, it should be clear that entering a marriage is one of the most important decisions you will ever make.

You can check with your healthcare insurance provider for

a list of counselors in your area. If you do not have a healthcare provider, you can search the Internet, the phone book, the library, or your city, county or state department of health. You can also ask family members and friends that you trust to make referrals.

If you can't get a meeting with a professional marriage counselor or can't afford it, you can buy books or videos on the topic of premarital advice. You can also find valuable information on the web. Another substitute for an actual counselor could be an older married couple or older person who has experience with being married. An older couple can help you to think through issues that they may have already encountered. Remember, though, that depending on their age, you may need to tweak their suggestions to apply to the current times. The person who has experience with marriage could be a divorcee, too. However, he or she should be pro-marriage. You want to hear from someone who is not bitter about having said "I do." They should want to share their experience to help you avoid their mistakes or pitfalls.

You can also receive counseling from your house of worship, free of charge. Many religious leaders require couples to receive counseling as a requirement to be married by the religious leader. There are advantages to having a pastoral counselor who can incorporate aspects of your faith, but also some disadvantages. If you believe marriage is a holy sacrament, then the counseling sessions can help you to see how you can live out your faith through your marriage. They can help you to see marriage as a form of worshiping God. This, in turn, can help you to see your spouse in a more spiritual light.

This said, people have a way of creating religious rules and practices that can cloud their ability to focus on hearing directly from God. As a Christian, I'm most familiar with what happens in churches, as opposed to temples or mosques, so I will speak about my experience only. I have seen church leaders use religion and traditions to place additional burdens on a marriage. Oftentimes, people read Scriptures literally or reinterpret Scriptures to fit their own agendas and beliefs. The problem is not God (or, if you prefer, The Creator), but people's manipulation of the Scriptures. If your faith-based counselor is making you feel that your marriage would put you in a state of bondage, then this could be a sign that you are not sitting before the correct counselor. For this reason, or if you do not follow a particular faith, the secular approach would likely be the better way for you.

COUNSELING TIME FRAME

You should start counseling as soon as possible to give yourself time to process what you've learned before going to the altar. Typically, sessions are held weekly and can last from one month to three months or more. The counseling could continue throughout the marriage depending on what the issues are. There is no specific rule.

Also, being engaged for at least a year or two and having premarital counseling during that time is a good idea. One of my "additional daughters" sought my advice on her relationship with her boyfriend who mentioned marriage but hadn't exactly popped the question. The boyfriend wanted her to move with him to another state across the country. They had already begun living together, so there was no sense in me trying to talk her out of that. However, during our heart-to-heart talk, I told her that she should move with him out of state as his fiancée only. I explained that being engaged would send a signal to both of them and everyone else that they weren't just a couple living together (*kickin' it*), but a couple with a mutual plan; they were moving toward their ultimate goal of being two committed individuals who are living as one.

"When you are out socially and he introduces you as his fiancée, trust me, you will feel much better about him and yourself in the relationship, and everyone will respect you both differently," I told her.

She smiled as she agreed with this idea and asked me to talk to her boyfriend about this as well. I met with him and we had "the talk" about his intentions. I told him how special a young lady that "my daughter" was to me and that if he loved her, he should ask her to marry him. "Make her your fiancée," I said.

I explained to him what I also said to her: They should take a year or two before marrying and they should both use the time to get joint premarital counseling and individual counseling.

They should not be afraid to learn so much about themselves and each other that they might decide to not get married at all.

"Would it be better to push ahead and marry and then learn that you weren't meant to be together, or would it be better to figure it out beforehand and go your separate ways and remain friends?"

He agreed, thanked me for "the talk" and we embraced. This was a couple of years ago. They eventually got married in another state in which they lived at the time. They invited me to their wedding reception in Virginia, which they flew back to so that more of their family members and friends could celebrate with them. They looked extremely happy together, dancing and sharing cake. As a photographer took photos of us, they said that they had taken my advice about premarital counseling. I didn't get a chance to hear from them how the counseling went, but they thanked me for giving them both "the talk."

A PASTOR'S STORY

A pastor friend shared with me that she insisted a couple that attends her church should receive counseling. Ironically, she was so insistent because the couple seemed so deeply in love. She feared that they might be relying too much on their passion for each other and were overlooking something important. The pastor was right.

As the couple attended the first counseling session, they stated that they didn't feel that they needed it. By the time they were done, they were extremely glad that they had gotten premarital counseling before taking the marriage plunge. When they began discussing their expectations, the man revealed that he was having an extremely hard time with the many hours that his fiancée's mother was spending at their home; in fact, she would stop by unannounced. Neither of them knew how to talk with the mother about this, and the resentment was building.

Close-knit family ties are fine if healthy, but this family was what counselors refer to as enmeshed. These are entangled relationships among family members where the boundaries are not clear. The mother would go through her daughter's and her fiancé's personal effects. The mother was intrusive, but she was merely doing what she was accustomed to doing. Prior to her future son-in-law moving in, the home had belonged exclusively to her daughter, and the mother's frequent visits had been the norm. After her future son-in-law's arrival, she had failed to make necessary adjustments with her visiting schedule. Meanwhile, her daughter failed to inform her mother that she needed to change. The daughter didn't know how to tell her mother this without thinking she would hurt her feelings. So the daughter ignored the elephant in the room while her fiancé's frustration simmered.

The man came from a family that was more individualistic. They rarely got together for weekend gatherings and certainly hadn't come together for a family reunion. That type of family closeness among his fiancée's clan was totally foreign to him and made him uncomfortable.

The counselor helped the daughter to assert herself in a loving way and helped her fiancé to be patient. The counselor helped them to see that there was no right or wrong, but that they just needed to develop their own comfort level of how to be together. They had to determine how they would teach, not only her mother, but all of her family members to observe certain boundaries. They would have to teach these lessons without anger.

The mother came to understand that she was overstepping her boundaries, and she eventually made the adjustment. The couple accomplished this by following the counselor's suggestion: They gave the mother, who was retired, a particular job to do on a regular basis to keep her busy and to help them out. The mother did the laundry. The mother was still at her daughter's house once a week, but not every day (and certainly not unannounced) as before.

Both individuals had brought something important to each other. The woman brought to her fiancé an understanding of family closeness that he hadn't known. The man brought to her an understanding of appropriate boundaries. The couple came back to the counselor a few months later before they were going to get married and thanked her.

RECAP

Premarital counseling is vital. By going through the 12 sessions recommended by professionally trained and credentialed counselors such as Bell, you and your marriage prospect can get on the same page about the most important issues that often doom marriages. Attending premarital counseling sessions should be as high a priority for you as would be studying to earn a driver's license so that you can drive an automobile. In order to drive legally, you have to first pass a test to get a learner's permit. You have to put in hours of actual practice to prepare for the road test. The practice is often done through professional driving schools. Finally, you have to pass a road test under the scrutiny of an expert evaluator before you're granted a license. In our society, we often prepare more for a driver's license than a marriage license. Common sense is not common.

I eloped and got married in Las Vegas (yup, Vegas). We arrived the previous night and slept in a hotel. The following morning, we walked across the street to the justice of the peace, and paid the fee for a marriage license. Rather than head to a chapel, we decided to exchange the vows there in the office. No premarital counseling. No simple equivalent of a learner's permit. Perhaps if there was counseling then, the secret that has caused my daughter, me, and the family so much pain would have come to light. Counseling or not, I had a right to know the whole truth before making my marriage decision.

CHAPTER 4

WHY IT'S NOT ALWAYS CHEAPER TO KEEP HER (OR HIM)

Dear Daughter,

A natural question that I get often from friends nowadays is: "Knowing what you know now, do you regret getting married?" My answer remains, "No." Regret is about feeling sad, repentant and disappointed for committing a wrong. I didn't do anything wrong to anyone by getting married, so why should I feel remorse? Besides, I don't regret it because, otherwise, I would not have experienced the joy of being your father. For example, I can remember coming home from tough days at work when I was a newspaper reporter. It can be a stressful career. You were a kindergartener then. You would meet me at the front door yelling, "Daddy, daddy, you're home!" and hug my knee. No one taught you to do that. It came natural to you. My stress would melt. Helping you and your brothers to grow and develop, and being there to help you navigate your ups and downs has been priceless. I am a better man and a better person because of it.

There are parents who are divorced or who have never married that manage to co-parent successfully as they share custody of their children. But for me, I could not picture myself NOT being there in the home raising you and your brothers. In large part, I know this came from my own childhood and the pain I felt when my parents divorced. Though your grandfather remained very involved in my life, I remember the deep void that I felt when he left our home. Like you, I was the youngest kid. A child feels safe and secure when daddy comes home. I didn't want you and your brothers to experience the insecurity that I endured. I didn't want you to have to grow up fast, like I did. So I tried to "make it work." In other words, I was wrestling with some "daddy issues." With that being said, though I dislike divorce, I know it's often necessary. I eventually realized that divorce was necessary for my parents. It was definitely necessary for me and your mother.

If you feel that a person is not contributing positively to your health and well-being, you must seriously consider ending the relationship—including if it's a marriage. You should weigh all of the costs—psychological, physical, spiritual and financial. Weigh the impact that it has on YOU first. If you fail to take care of yourself, you won't be much good to the people who would be depending on you, such as your children who did not ask to be brought into the situation. Then, ponder seriously the impact on them. Too often, adults make selfish decisions that wound powerless children. Too often, parents who are at odds intentionally use their children as weapons. Yes, children are resilient and could recover, but the wounds of collateral damage *can be very slow to heal. Sometimes this can't be avoided, but it can ALWAYS be minimized. Daughter, please hear me that when it comes to the question of divorce, whether you have children or not, ALWAYS make the decision that is ultimately in YOUR best interest going forward. Pray for guidance. So, no, I do not regret my decision to marry. I still believe in the institution of marriage. We've also had many good family moments, as you know, and you and your brothers have been a blessing. The key to marriage is preparing yourself ahead of time and discovering the right person for the right reasons. Likewise, I also made the right decision to divorce, despite the tremendous costs. It led to uncovering the truth that has set you and me free. No regrets, no shame.*

"Cheaper to Keep Her" is a song by "The Philosopher of Soul" Johnnie Taylor. Sung to a slow drag dance beat, Taylor basically urges (and warns) married men that they're better off staying with their wives, or else face paying a lot of alimony, child support, or even spending time in jail. Here's one of Taylor's classic lines:

You didn't pay but two dollars to bring the little girl home

Now you're about to pay two thousand to leave her alone

You see another woman out there and you want to make a change

She ain't gonna want you 'cause you won't have a damn thing

That's why it's cheaper to keep her (Everybody sing along with me) It's cheaper to keep her (it's cheaper to keep her) . . .

Taylor's advice to men is definitely wise, but I actually disagree with him somewhat. For the purposes of this book, let's also realize that it's not always cheaper to keep HIM either. In states like Virginia, where I live, both spouses are equally responsible for supporting each other financially. Each partner, whether man or woman, can be eligible for child support and alimony, too. Alimony is typically set aside for a spouse who was restricted from having a career and earning an income because their main job was working inside of the home rearing children. (Yes, rearing children is definitely work!) Alimony is intended not as punishment, but to ease the spouse's financial transition to being single.

You may be asking yourself why I'm bringing up the topic of financial costs associated with divorce in a book that provides premarital counseling. It's because a lot of couples only consider the costs of getting married and staying married. It's important to understand everything you're getting into when you enter the state of marriage, because in this country with its high divorce rate, divorce is just as much a potential reality as going through with your wedding. Best to know all that may lie ahead—the negative and positive—as you decide to marry the one you're with. This chapter will explore the costs of divorce and other financial topics.

THE COSTS OF MARRIAGE (AHEM) DIVORCE

Back to Taylor's song. He is correct that if one spouse splits, the paying of alimony and child support will likely be painful. Writing that monthly check without having control over how it gets spent will likely give you a monthly twitch, especially if you do not have regular visitation with your children. But child support should not be a problem because any parent should want to do the right thing by their children. Now, alimony? That's another thing altogether. If you don't feel the spouse is deserving of it, there's gonna be an angry signature on that check. If your spouse was not working outside of the home (and could have been working but declined), you're going to feel as though they're getting a windfall for sitting home all day and watching TV in between posting selfies on social media websites.

It's curious as to how someone like this, who was no longer rearing young children, nor consistently involved in building the family's wealth, would insist on receiving alimony. Why not just divvy up each other's belongings and go your separate ways? Nonetheless, women and men present themselves publicly as independent and self-sufficient, yet privately insist on alimony from their ex-spouse to finance their public persona. This is apparently what they call a financial planning strategy. Gold digging is gender neutral.

    The good news is that prior to 2018, alimony was tax-deductible for the payer. The receiver has to pay taxes on it. If you were carrying your spouse financially for years anyway, at least through the alimony payments, you get to write off some of that expense if you itemize your deductions. But God help you if the judge decides you've got to pay alimony for a lifetime. Sorry, I don't have any advice for dealing with that. On another note, child support is not tax-deductible, and should not be. If you're angry about writing a check for a child that you brought into this world or that you adopted, you've got a bigger problem that needs fixing. Basically, you're a jerk or *jerkette*.

    I also disagree with Taylor somewhat because peace of mind is priceless. Is it better to stay in a frustrating marriage that is like one or two dead people walking? Is it better to be on an "un-merry-go-'round" visiting the same tired issues over and over and over? I believe in "until death do us part," but if the marriage dies before either of the two individuals do, then let the death of the marriage "do us part." Both individuals ought to be wise enough to end the misery. It's better to part ways in order to breathe and live life to its fullest, than to drown slowly in an unhappy marriage. I agree with the lyrics written by the British rock star and songwriter Sting:

> *If you need somebody, call my name*
> *If you want someone, you can do the same*
> *If you want to keep something precious*
> *You got to lock it up and throw away the key*
> *If you want to hold onto your possession*
> *Don't even think about me*
> *If you love somebody, set them free*

MARRIAGE: THE FINANCIAL AND HISTORICAL ORIGINS

Marriage is almost as old as humans and comes in all types of shapes and sizes across the world. In America, we basically have three models: rationalistic (We are compatible and can mutually benefit each other. Let's form a union!); romantic (You are the love of my life. You make my mornings and my nights. Will you marry me, Darling?); and Judeo-Christian (The Lord chose you for me. Let's honor God and raise godly children together).

In more recent times in the United States, same-sex marriage has also taken its place on the historic stage. It became legal for the first time in May 2004 in Massachusetts, and other states began slowly opening their courthouse doors (In 2013, Timothy Bostic, one of my former university professors, became the principal plaintiff in Bostic v. Schaefer, which challenged Virginia's ban on same-sex marriage). In 2015 the United States Supreme Court ruled 5-4 that the Constitution guarantees a right to same-sex marriage in all 50 states.

For many in America, marriage is a legal agreement rooted in love, where individuals pledge to care for each other forever. For many others, it's more spiritual and religious-based. Books of faith offer "The Way" that marriage can and should work, but since these tomes are often misinterpreted, many people end up on the wrong path. Whether secular or religious, "I do" means you are pledging to submit to a shared cause that's greater than each individual, yet should also be mutually beneficial to each individual. You are a team, yet you are also key players with individual needs to be nourished. As I've said before, you don't want to be stuck trying to "make work" this balancing act, and may I add, especially not in today's "What's in it for me?" society where no-fault divorces make breaking up easy to do. To avoid divorce, you need the mindset and the tools to "let it work." Otherwise, I say stay single and in love with yourself. Plenty of people are happy being single. They enjoy the company of others on their own terms minus the stress that a bad marriage can cause. Living single beats sleeping with the enemy!

Now, let's look at some of the ways money and a couple's differing attitudes toward it can impact a marriage, and why these differences need to be settled before you tie the knot. The consequences of not doing so are summed up perfectly by this next sentence:

Be on the same page about working and money or don't get married, because you won't be happy and likely won't stay married.

As stated in Chapter 2, it is imperative that you and your potential spouse see eye-to-eye on issues such as whether one or both of you works and how you manage your family's money. If you don't, you're setting yourself up for major marriage problems. If you're not on the same page about working and money management, this is a good time to explore the downsides and benefits of the various ways of running the company that could become The Two of You, Inc. Simply put, debates about work and income are among the key reasons why marriages fail. Because of stagnant income growth and the tough economic downturn that began in 2007, income issues are putting tremendous pressure on marriages.

Prior to the 1970s, one spouse, typically the husband, could make enough money to take care of a family of four on one blue-collar job. Today, many of these jobs have been shipped overseas where labor is cheaper. Factories have closed and the jobs have gone away, never to return in large part because of automation. Meanwhile, despite this new normal, American culture in the early 21st century still operates very much on the 1950s gender role values in regard to income when it comes to male and female pairings.

Many men and women still believe that the husband ought to be out pulling the highest income, while the wife should be home nurturing the children. Husbands, who are unable to generate enough income to solely support the entire family, often return home to resentful wives. Forced out into the workplace (where women often STILL make less than men in the same jobs), many of these wives may feel that if their husbands were more successful, they, the wives, would be able to remain home. For these women, fatherhood is still valued based on the paycheck system. Men are basically expected to generate enough income to be the sole breadwinner or to pay child support in order to meet their obligations. This creates a major problem for men who are out of work because of the rapidly changing economy, though under these circumstances, men obviously contribute much more to the rearing of children. A University of London study found that fathers spend seven times more time with their children today than they did in the 1970s—35 minutes per day compared to five minutes daily. Meanwhile, working mothers were found to spend one hour per day compared to 15 minutes.

People who feel financial distress are more divorce prone. Parents need to be valued beyond just a paycheck. Being a working parent can put strains on the marriage, especially if spouses have to work more than one job. Moving around the country for better job opportunities can also isolate people from their family support system. If you're middle- to upper-middle class or higher, remaining in one community is ideal but often unrealistic because relocating for jobs often is required to increase or maintain salary levels. Poor people are less likely to move out of a community, but they are more likely to live in a deteriorating community. Watching the community fall apart around you increases your stress and strains marriages. Lack of opportunities also creates despair. To survive and thrive in this new normal economic environment requires a quick attitude/values adjustment. Unfortunately, this is often difficult to accomplish because people are typically adverse to change.

But if you seek to enter into a marriage on a successful footing, you have to be open to that change and so does your potential spouse. It can't be stressed enough: It all starts with being on the same page about money-related matters. The big ones involve how the family money is spent, whether to maintain separate bank accounts, and who will work outside the home. You'll need to agree on all these matters. Let's take a look.

SEEING EYE-TO-EYE ON WORKING AND MONEY

Some ways to be on the same page about working and money are to explore the benefits of various ways of handling each. Let's start first with how you and your potential spouse may deal with bank accounts.

Bank Accounts—Separate or Joint?

Personally, I believe in couples having both joint and individual bank accounts. This approach encourages cooperation and trust. The joint account fosters the unity necessary to be "the partnership of one," while the individual account supports the trust and individuality that married couples should maintain. If income for both married individuals is primarily from working a job, consider having all of the income directly deposited into the joint account—one pot. In this way, you both see all of the money and have access to all of the marriage income. Then apply the 70-30/3 Rule. This rule means that you devote 70 percent to the household expenses (mortgage, food, utilities, etc.), then divide the remaining 30 percent (10 percent tithes and/or donations, 10 percent savings, 10 percent individual allowances). Again, all the money goes into the one pot—the joint account—and then flows to the other necessary areas, including allowances into the individual accounts.

It is from individual accounts that both marriage partners get to do whatever they want with their allowances. Do you want to go on a golfing trip to Brazil with your college buddies? Your individual account is where the money should come from. Do you want to fly to the Caribbean for spa weekend? Don't pull out a credit card; pull out the debit card from your separate individual account to finance the trip. If either of you needs a little extra money for personal use, just talk it through and take it from the joint account.

If one of the individuals receives a financial windfall (a bonus, a gift, heck!—wins the lottery), the first consideration should be what the household account needs (partnership of one) to go into the joint account pot. After that, there should be no problem if the spouse puts the money directly into their personal individual account (trust and individuality).

Another major consideration as you determine how family finances will be addressed is to decide who will run "the family business," The Two of You, Inc. Every company needs a head officer.

Who Will Be The Family's COO?

One person should be the main individual—the chief operating officer—who manages the family's finances. This person should report to their partner what is going on with the family's money. The report could be monthly or quarterly, whatever you both decide. Both individuals should have equal access to the joint accounts, but you can't have two people managing the money and making withdrawals because confusion will seep in. In a company or organization, there is a reason why you typically have one accountant or finance department that reports to the rest of the body. One person managing the finances in a transparent way encourages efficiency and, most importantly, trust.

This is not a rigid, robotic rule. The ratios can be adjusted (80/20 or 60/40, for example) to meet the couple's needs. Some couples believe in keeping all accounts separate and paying their own bills separately. If this method works for both of the individuals involved, they should go with it. The point is having a clear understanding of how you BOTH want to manage the financial matters of your marriage. It helps, however, to have a company leader.

Who Will Go To Work?

Another major issue you must agree on: deciding who will work in or outside of the home. You and your potential spouse MUST be on the same page on this one before formally committing to one another.

Most of what follows addresses the challenges married couples have faced for decades over the question, "Who will go to work?"

Who works and where has, for what seems like eons now, related to whether the man would feel comfortable if his wife made more money. First, being the primary caregiver of the children in the home IS work. In fact, being the COO of the family is vital and deserving of high praise. If the family can afford it, one parent should remain in the home in order to focus more (not alone) on child rearing. And this parent could be either spouse. There are married women CEOs of Fortune 500 companies. There are married women who are running small businesses. In these cases, the husbands are at home being the family's COO. As for me, "Go make that money, Babe. Daddy is staying home with the children!" is what I would say if my wife were a CEO for a major company and we were rearing young children! But if the family can't afford to live financially on one salary, both spouses should be equally involved in working in and outside of the home.

As for who makes more, I personally would not have a problem if my wife made more than me (This was far from the case, however). The more the merrier. Other men see this differently. Being the sole breadwinner, as the wife stays home with the kids, is crucial to their self-esteem. Despite the expansion of career opportunities, some career women are tired of having to work every day and desire to stay home. That's fine, too, as long as both husband and wife are on the same page about this. I would have a problem with a marriage prospect that COULD work, but did not want to. I would have a problem if she ACTED like she was seriously looking for a job, but secretly sabotaged every opportunity that presented itself to her, especially if the point of the income was to save for the children's college and or our retirement; this IS definitely a deal breaker for me.

A counselor that I know told me she has noticed a trend among many young working women. They are planning to quit their jobs when they get married, but the men they are engaged to have no clue about this. Again, there's nothing wrong with not wanting to work outside of the home. Raising a child and managing a home IS work. Being dishonest is what's wrong here. Take this prime example of a couple who mirrored this very notion: The woman had worked nearly 10 years in the medical industry and was making a good salary. However, while in an individual session, she revealed that she planned to get pregnant, quit her job, and stay at home with the baby. She said she was "tired of working all these years." She didn't say it outright, but it was clear that to her, the husband's role was to take care of her 'til death did them part. "Yeah, and her husband would be the one to die an early death," the counselor said. Disturbed by this, the counselor asked the woman if her fiancé was on board with her plan. The woman sat back in her seat, rolled her neck, and said, "He doesn't know."

Hmmm. Planting the seeds of divorce, maybe?

Meanwhile, her fiancé had a similarly long career in corporate management and was making a good salary. However, he was concerned about what it would take to get and maintain the American dream—owning a $300,000 or more valued home in a great suburban neighborhood with great schools that their future children would attend. He was thinking that he might need to take on more debt to pursue an MBA degree to increase his earnings potential. While his future wife was plotting not to work, he was depending on combining their salaries—turn two good incomes into one great family income. It was a classic setup for a marriage that they would spend years trying to "make work."

Of course, women do not have a monopoly on this "I don't want to work anymore" mentality. Many more women are in the workforce compared to previous generations. Unfortunately, there are a lot of men who have grown up with parents who gave them nearly every material possession their little boy hearts desired. The $150 to $200 Nike Air Jordan sneakers? Got it. The nearly $1,000 video game console with all of the expensive accessories? Got it. Over the years, these little boys grew up believing that someone is supposed to take care of them ('til death do them part), rather than being responsible adults who take care of themselves. Instead of a responsible man, the boy grows into a man-child—an immature mind in a mature body. A pastor told me that when she and her husband counsel troubled married couples and the wife is complaining that she is "not trying to raise a grown man," it's usually because she is married to a man-child.

The way I see it, both the husband and wife should work if they can each physically and mentally hold down a job. The median household income for a typical American family of four is about $56,516 based on 2015 U.S. Census figures. This number had been rather stagnant since 1989, but was up 5.2% the previous year. Today's economy remains unfriendly to most one-income families. On such an income or less, it is very difficult to cover a mortgage, two car payments, and all of the family's other bills, while also saving for college and retirement (Remember, based on 2015 dollars, it cost an estimated $233.610 to raise a child to age 18). Under these circumstances, for a woman or man to go into a marriage "looking for a sponsor" and plotting NOT to work is not only selfish, it's just plain criminal.

In a family that is financially well off and secure on one spouse's income, this is obviously less of an issue. However, the other spouse should still have something outside of the home that they are focused on. They should consider doing volunteer work for an organization or a cause that they're passionate about. For me, I would prefer my wife have something important to her going on that I can be supportive of in the way that I would want her to be supportive of my career and outside interests. It's healthy for the relationship for me to accompany her to an event that's in her professional and or social world, and be referred to as "Miss Thing's husband." If it's always the other way around, individual identity insecurities could ease in. Besides, in a long-term relationship, you're going to need something more to enjoy together than sex and rearing children. At some point, both will come to an end. You are going to need to be able to talk to each other about your goals and aspirations. It's a shame if all a woman or man has to offer a spouse is their sex organ. For every highly attractive woman you see, there's likely a man who is tired of having sex with her, and vice versa.

Working is not just about money; it's actually more about being aligned with your life's purpose. Whether working for income or volunteering, getting up and focusing on something other than yourself can make you a better-rounded person. It keeps you in touch with your spouse's world because your own outside world experience will provide insight regarding the issues your spouse deals with daily at work. It can keep you from becoming an obnoxious narcissist, someone who is insecure and who craves attention from everyone around them.

A marriage is about individuals who have a purpose that they are both helping each other nurture and realize. When both spouses have an individual interest they are involved in, it actually fosters that sense of the value of "the partnership of one" and being a team player. Meanwhile, it empowers their individual identities. Why? Because when people meet you, they typically ask, "What do you do?" Not everyone has matured to the level of enlightenment to understand that just being interconnected with nature, living in the moment, and enhancing the lives of others we come in contact with *is* enough of an answer! Particularly in America and Western cultures we want to impress and be proud of our answer concerning what we do career-wise or what causes we are involved in. We want our spouses to be proud of our answer, too, because spouses represent each other.

Spouses who don't work in the home, but rather *just stay* home and watch mindless TV all day in between posting selfies on social media will eventually find their thoughts rambling in foolishness. They won't understand when their "better half" needs to put in extra hours at work to accomplish a major revenue generating project. They will pout if you tell them that you're going to an industry networking reception; instead of realizing that this is crucial to developing contacts that can boost your career, they will conjure in their minds that you're having an extramarital affair. If you invite them to join you, they may tell you that it's too far for them to drive and that they don't like to drive in urban traffic, and that you should just come home. After months or years of this type of aggravation, perhaps you eventually *will* have an affair with someone who on the surface seems to be more compatible than your spouse. An individual's mind can convince itself and justify just about anything. Locked in "making it work" mode, you'll tell yourself that stepping outside of the marriage is OK because you work hard and deserve a doctor who can make you feel good. The idle and frustrated minds of spouses are both mere playgrounds for the devil. A failure of couples to be on one accord about working and money can certainly unearth the roots of mischief that brings about bad karma.

RECAP

Overall, I'm in the camp of those who believe marriage is a covenant. It shouldn't be a contract that you easily break if you feel things aren't going the way you like anymore. But there comes a point when staying in a marriage that isn't working *is* too costly. To me, peace of mind is priceless. So, no, as I see it, it's not always *cheaper to keep her or him*. But one way you can avoid the hassle and heartache of divorce is by ensuring that you and your potential spouse are in agreement on the big financial questions of marriage *before* you become husband and wife.

The song, "It's Cheaper to Keep Her," is definitely wise advice for many marriage situations, but as I've pointed out in this chapter, not always accurate. So please, please, please, work out ahead of time how you will manage the family's finances, so that you and your spouse don't wind up on the road to divorce and having to determine whether it *really is cheaper to keep her or him.*

CHAPTER 5

YOUR LIFE WILL NO LONGER BE YOUR OWN ... CAN YOU HANDLE THAT?

Dear Daughter,

Over the years I've talked to you a lot about being a confident woman who knows who she is as an individual. I've tried to nurture you to be a "virtuous woman," like the one written about in the Bible, in the book of Proverbs 31. As you know, what I love about this wife is that she has clearly maintained her individuality. She embodies the traditional and modern woman. She is a mother who is very attentive to her home. "She watches over the affairs of her household and does not eat the bread of idleness. Her children arise and call her blessed; her husband also, and he praises her . . . " She is a businesswoman who "considers a field and buys it; out of her earnings she plants a vineyard . . . She sees that her trading is profitable, and her lamp does not go out at night." Clearly, she can stand on her own without her husband, yet she compliments him. "Her husband has full confidence in her and lacks nothing of value. She brings him good, not harm, all the days of her life." They are true partners. She is the type of wife who stands by her husband as they take on the world together. She would never undermine him in their home, especially when it comes to their children honoring him. She is the type of mother who empowers her children with the confidence to go after their dreams to the full. She is a role model to her sons and particularly a great role model to her daughters. I am proud to say that this is the type of woman that I see coming of age within you.

One of the things that I find so special about this biblical passage is that it is actually the words of a mother (like my late mom—your Abuela) advising her son on the type of woman that he should marry. You know that your grandma adored you. She's watching over both of us. Who could be more qualified to define "finer womanhood" than another woman who is wise? The Scripture doesn't say whether the "Proverbs 31 Woman" had a loving relationship with her dad. I'm willing to bet that if not her dad, there was another positive older male role model somewhere in her life, perhaps a nurturing loving grandfather.

On my radio show, Dr. Carletta N. Perry, a professional counselor and psychology professor based in Virginia, was rather blunt regarding why so many people are divorcing: They just aren't ready to get married.

"It's not the institution of marriage that is the issue," Perry said. "The institution hasn't changed—it's the person. Are you going into the marriage for the right reason? What's your agenda?"

Many people pretend to be something they are not, Perry says, like putting more effort into their appearance prior to marriage and then letting things slide dramatically afterward.

Because so many people are ill-prepared for tying the knot and put up a façade along the path of "reeling in the fish," they can't possibly be ready for the individual adjustments they're going to need to make if they expect the marriage to succeed.

This chapter explores ways your life may change after you say "I do." If you recognize you're not ready or don't want your life to mirror any of these scenarios, it's probably best not to put a ring on it yet.

THE ONENESS OF MARRIAGE

It is an unfortunate fact that in many cultures (including during Colonial times in America), for generations, wives have been treated as the property of their husbands. So the idea of submission or sharing your body can be extremely off-putting if viewed only in that context. In Western cultures, such as in America (though sexual abuse is alarmingly high), the idea of your individual body being community property is foreign compared to many other societies, because we believe in rugged individualism and individual rights. So when it comes to intimacy between two people and how they share and view each other's bodies, this can cause a complicated dance, especially in a marriage. For example, if you like her hair long, what happens if she decides to cut it? What if he decides to change his hair color to blond or red? What if one or the two of you put on a lot of weight? There are other issues like these that at first glance may seem trivial and/or easy to overcome, but trust me on this—none of these are to be underestimated in the context of marriage.

Midlife Man-O-Pause

Sex is obviously the key area in which married couples share their bodies. We've covered that in some detail in Chapter 3, "Warning Signs," so, here, let's consider a different illustration to make this point: body art.

At one of my early newspaper jobs, a colleague launched into a rant about her 50-something-year-old husband and his tattoos. They had been married more than 25 years and were newly empty nesters. The husband had always wanted a tattoo, so now that their youngest child had gone away for college, he decided it was time to get one. My colleague was OK with her husband getting a tattoo; she shared that she herself had gotten a tattoo of a rose on her right rib when she was 16 (no, she didn't show it to us). Hers was a rebellious act at the time. After college and during her late 20s, she went through a phase where she was embarrassed by it and wanted it removed. But then considering the permanent mark that would remain, she decided, "What the heck. Just keep it. Only my husband sees it, and he likes it."

My colleague went along with her husband to the tattoo parlor. He picked out three tattoos and she told him the one that she liked the best. It was an anchor with a boat because he liked to sail. They would often sail together and planned to sail even more now that the kids were gone. Without her knowing, it turned out to be the same "best tattoo" that her husband had in mind, so that was all the confirmation that he needed to do it. She watched as he got the tattoo on the left side of his chest. They joked through the process, especially when he winced from the pain. He was happy with it. She liked it. The experience was fun. Her husband was now sporting *their* tattoo. When they would make love, she would clutch the tattoo on his chest. Of course the story doesn't end there, though. Her husband soon had 10 tattoos and counting!

"I don't get it!" she said. "What the hell. It's like he's having some type of midlife crisis or something. It's like . . . it's like . . . something else is going on. One was fine, maybe two, but all these tattoos? It's such a distraction, a turnoff."

Apparently, she didn't know which tattoo to clutch, so there hadn't been much clutching going on between them lately. She said that she was somewhat turned off from sex. Actually, what my colleague was most upset about was that she didn't have any participation in the subsequent tattoos. She was not consulted like she had been during the first one. To my colleague, the additional tattoos were all about her husband.

"They were all about *his* body, not *our* body," she said.

Though your body *is* your temple, if you're in a true "partnership of one" marriage, you are sharing your body with your mate. You maintain your individuality, but like in the community-oriented cultures that I mentioned earlier, you are also sharing with the community. You are committing your body to another person as they commit theirs to you for a greater common good that enhances both of your lives. This is by no means servitude or submission, like slavery or prostitution. It is about two individuals willingly sharing themselves with one another. Therefore, married couples should not make major permanent decisions about their individual bodies without at least consulting their mates. Consultation is NOT about asking for the other person's permission. Your body is "still your thing" and you can do what you want to do with it. Being married means you recognize and respect the "partnership of one" that you've both willingly agreed to. This means you are mutually considerate of each other's needs and desires. You represent each other. You share your bodies with each other.

People get tattoos in all types of areas of their bodies. If your spouse is fine with this without consultation, then great. Go for it. But if you know that your spouse is really not into such things, why would you go rogue and get the tattoos without at least consulting them? Even if the artwork is not visible to the general public, doesn't your partner have to experience it?

Say a wife puts across her back a tattoo which spells out some type of philosophical quote. She knows that her husband, though not totally against tattoos, is not a huge fan either. Say the husband prefers modesty. In order to see the quote regularly, the wife has to look in the mirror in the bathroom and read it backward, right? What is the true message then? Is it that someone else has (or is) back there *reading* when the husband is not around? Oh, no, check that . . . the goal is for the tattoo to be seen during the summer while wearing a bikini on the beach, right? Either way, who is that tattoo truly for, if the husband isn't into it? Could there be just a tiny bit of narcissism and seeking attention from others going on here? Again, if your spouse is fine without being consulted, no problem. But if not . . .

And when it comes to visible tattoos, if, for example, the husband truly understands the potential negative income impact of his sporting of a tattoo that can be observed while he is interviewing for a good paying job, what message is he truly sending to his wife concerning his desire to work? He has been out of work for more than three years, but he is *still getting tattoos*? Is he more concerned about his individual expression than he is about the health and welfare of his family? Does he expect his wife to foot all of the household bills until death does *she* part?

Again, it's not about whether tattoos are good or bad. Tattoos are just a real example. My point is that you and your potential mate should agree before you marry about how you will share your bodies with each other and display your bodies to the outside world. And if there are changes along the way—like what happened with my newsroom colleague and her husband—you should consult with your spouse first and not go rogue. And when you discuss things like this make sure that you are honest. Personally, to me, there are few things more frustrating than a woman who says what she thinks her husband wants to hear, rather than what she truly believes. A woman who nods, "Yes" indicating that we have an important mutual understanding, only to go off on her own later and do the opposite of what we agreed upon.

Let's look at some other ways in which your life is no longer your own after you marry. Again, the key question here is, are you ready for this?

***Becoming a Parent**. First, of course, you and your spouse will need to determine if you both want children and, if so, how many. (See Chapter 2, "Warning Signs," for a previous treatment of the topic.) If you're both in accord on the answers to those questions, just remember as a married couple with children, not only will your lives belong to one another, but they will also belong to your children. Children do not ask to come into the world, so it will be up to you to make sure they have what they need to lead successful lives.

Oftentimes, the thing children need most from you is your presence. They need to know who their parents are to help them secure their own sense of identity. You need to engage them and guide them on their level and the activities that they are interested in. Play video games with them or hang out with them at the monkey bars on the playground. This will be one of the few times in life that you can behave like a kid and not look silly, so embrace it.

Children are a blessing (I'm thankful that I committed to rearing mine), but they can also cause a tremendous amount of pain as they take your emotions to unexpected realms. A Princeton University/Stony Brook University study on adult happiness published in 2014, surveyed 1.8 million Americans. Among them were parents between ages 34 and 46. The study found that parents tended to experience more highs and lows than their childless counterparts. So if you seriously want children, be ready for the rollercoaster ride that may not necessarily be a great adventure. A relative of mine who is a mother of three has been recently suggesting to friends and anyone who will listen that they think seriously about having only one child or none at all. Think of the benefits of, for example, being able to call your spouse and say, "Hey, let's fly to New Orleans for the weekend"—without having to worry about a babysitter or rushing home if your child gets seriously ill.

Lastly, here is a very important message to wives and mothers that many husbands and fathers know: You have more power over the minds of your children than their fathers do. Much of this is because of the magical birth bond that you share, or if adopted, it will be because mothers tend to spend more nurturing time with children due to culture norms. The dad can be the most responsible man who is worthy of honor and being modeled and respected by his children. But if mom signals to the children that they don't have to listen to him, the children likely won't. The signals can be, and often are, subtle. For example, the father can say, "Finish your chores and your homework project before you go out and play." If when the dad is in his man cave, the mom actually does the chores and the assignment at the kitchen table, what message does this send to the children? Meanwhile, the dad returns, sees that his directive was *apparently* been completed, but doesn't know that his leadership and role model position in the household is steadily being undermined. Eventually, the children become teenagers (aliens) and they may begin openly disrespecting their dad in *his* world—the home he's paying for—as if *they* own it. They begin mastering their deception tactics learned from their mom. They lie to their dad. Either way, the battle begins, but the dad does not know what the source is. He does not realize he has been sleeping with the enemy. The children will become the collateral damage as they struggle to reach their full potential. They may grow up "liking" the mom more as they continue calling her "mommy" even through their teens and young adult years. Mom may enjoy the temporary benefits of being their "friend." But in the end, the children will have a warped view of the world, how it truly works in terms of the need for hard work and discipline, and they will likely struggle to find their place as adults. Here's the thing: Even if the dad is a "My way or the highway" tyrant who rules with fear, the children won't buy into it unless their mother cosigns by being an enabler!

Another way women warp their own children's development is by venting to them about their dad. Parental disputes are inevitable, but to seek an ally in the child hurts the child. This often happens during a divorce, as parents seek sympathy for their position in the failed relationship that has nothing to do with the child. Don't do it. The child (perhaps adult children even more so) already feels as though she is in the middle and having to choose a side. Stop the mental assault! Mothers have overriding power in the household. So work together with your children's father regarding the key issues that will help the children to become successful, healthy adults. Be a united front for your children's own good. Don't undermine your husband thinking that you're reaping some personal gain. Daughters and sons need certain specifics from their father that a mother can't give and vice versa. Ultimately your children will suffer the loss and the pain because of you.

***Career Ambitions**. You may still be able to achieve or work in the career you had wanted, but if a career opportunity arises in a place where your spouse and/or kids don't want to move to, you may find yourself stuck with your current employer. In short, getting married may mean you will need to stifle or limit the scope of your career dreams in order to keep your family as the main priority.

Uprooting your family from city to city can take a toll. One of my children attended three different high schools because of career moves I made. Meanwhile, all of my career changes were made to benefit the family because I was the main breadwinner and needed to increase our income. I also turned down an ideal job with a prominent media company back in my hometown of New York City because that's not where their mother and I thought it was best to raise our family. Staying put and growing your career where you are may have its limits, but it may not be a bad idea. Taking a job in another state while your family stays behind can take a toll and certainly tear up your marriage.

***Discretionary Spending.** Things that you were able to buy for yourself when you were single may become no-no's due to family financial constraints. When you're married, and especially if you plan to or already have children, you need to put money toward them. The extra money you have could go toward college savings, or your emergency fund to cover the needs of the extra people you are now responsible for.

If you are serious about nurturing your children's development, you're going to want them to have the broadest experiences possible. They may want, for example, to get involved in sports. My children were all into track and field when they were 12 years old and younger. We traveled the country with them every summer. There may be piano or violin lessons. There may be dance recitals or martial arts tournaments. How about summer camp? You may want them to have those experiences. Maybe even go to private school.

These extra activities cost money—lots of money over time. Unless the family is wealthy and money is not a concern, chances are both parents will need to make good salaries to cover these important extracurricular costs. This means something is going to have to give that you likely would've bought when you were single. Perhaps you can't go on golfing trips with your buddies as frequently. Perhaps you and your sister friends can't fly out each year to New Orleans for the annual music festival. You work hard for your money and you deserve to buy yourself an expensive suit or designer bag, but the needs of your children will cause you to have to make major sacrifices. After all, they didn't ask for you to birth them into this world.

***Friends.** If all of your friends are single, you're likely going to have to trade most of them in for friends who are married. Single people will tend to want to do what single people do, which is, for the most part, the old stuff that you stopped wanting to do once you got on the road to getting married. Look through the windshield, not in the rearview mirror. If your single friends can't ride with you in your new car, then you've got to let them out.

RECAP

Getting married will change you. Essentially, you're getting married because you want to share yourself and grow with another person. You are essentially saying that you WANT to change, so expect to change. If you're going into the marriage expecting to behave exactly as you did when you were single, then make sure your spouse is on board. If that arrangement works for both of you, then go for it. But it does beg the question: If both of you want to join in a partnership with each other, but remain exactly the same as if you were single, then why get married? Why not just remain friends?

As Dr. Carletta N. Perry pointed out, too many people get married without being ready. They don't have a clue of what they're getting into and why, which is one of the key reasons why the divorce rate is high. They go into marriage with personal agendas. Marriage is about two individuals coming together to create a single unit that benefits them both. Marriage is about sharing your bodies and representing each other in the community. Your individual life will no longer be an individual life after you marry, so come aboard and enjoy the voyage. If you're not serious about this, save yourself the hassles of the trip by paddling your separate ways now.

CHAPTER 6

THE POWER OF EMPATHY

To my Daughters and Sons,

This may sound odd to you, but you can be successfully married to someone without loving them. You can also love more than one person at the same time, which is a reason why married people also cheat. Therefore, you should tone down the talk about being in love with a person unless you are positive that you understand what love truly is. Many people use the word "love" loosely, but they really don't grasp it because they're not mature enough yet. That's not intended to be a slight to young adults. There are middle-aged people who are immature. Focus instead on being empathetic first. That's easier to do, much more reliable and could lead you to mature love that can last.

I believe empathy, the ability to feel for yourself what another person is feeling, is the key component necessary for a successful

> marriage partnership. Empathy is key to friendship. Empathy fuels that friendship as you see the reflections of your personhood in each other's eyes as you face life together and cover each other's backs. With constant practice, eventually, empathy will become natural to you—your first instinct when dealing with your mate. As you exercise empathy regularly, it will strengthen your ability to tap into "godly love." This love is deeper and more sustaining than romantic love, which you can "fall out of." Godly love requires spiritual muscles. It means you will sacrifice for your mate. It compels you to be honest and selfless, yet enables you to STILL prioritize your own needs. You won't obsess over your lover and lose yourself. Instead, you will mutually want the best for each other and will commit to doing what it takes to achieve it—even if that means letting go. It's true that love can sustain your relationship during the worst of storms. It can inspire you to choose to forgive. Empathy can lead you to love as it keeps the relationship floating on a day-to-day basis. Basically, I'm telling you that love is complex. It's not the simple fairy tale fantasy that we're typically fed in pop culture. Study love first before you commit to it, and practice empathy daily. Empathy is the key that can open you to true unconditional love.

When I look at my adult children, none of whom (at the writing of this book) are yet married, I see young people who have a chance to "do marriage well" that is, without unnecessary pain from beginning to end. Fortunately for them, I have spent many years cleaning my dirty laundry, figuring out my mistakes, and pouring out knowledge about marriage and relationships that, if my children are receptive to my experiences and my message, should help them avoid many of the ditches (remember "codependence" was one?) it took me years to dig myself out from.

That said, my divorce from their mother has not been easy for them even though they were already adults when it happened. A misconception is that adult children are able to handle their parents' divorce easier because they are more mature. In fact, because they truly understand the ramifications, adult children may take the divorce harder. Adding to the pain, the parents often involve their adult children in the divorce mess. The adult children often feel that they are in the middle and have to choose a side. Unsolicited comments from a miserable grandmother or aunt in the peanut gallery is added salt to the wounds. However, I hope that my children would take the best of what they observed growing up and apply it to their own marriages should they ever walk down the aisle. But even more than all of that, I would hope that they take to heart this critical key point about how to *allow* a marriage to work.

Let's now take a look at the power of empathy.

The Power of Empathy to Unlock the Door to a Happy, Sustained Marriage

Empathy is essentially the Golden Rule: Treat others the way that you want to be treated. It is deeper than sympathy, which is having compassion, but not necessarily feeling enough to be moved to take action. You don't even have to be in love with someone to act on empathy. For example, you can see a homeless person on the street that you don't know and have empathy for them. You buy them something to eat. You can see that a coworker needs help finishing a project, so you step in and lend a hand. You do these things, not necessarily out of devoted love (though many people do love their neighbors as they love themselves), but because you feel what the other person is feeling, you connect with them. The action you take is what you'd hope someone would do for you if you were in need. Likewise, when a challenge arises in your relationship (and it definitely will), you simply think about how you might feel if you were in your spouse's shoes. You think about what your needs might be and then act accordingly. If more relationships relied on empathy (the ability to feel and identify with another person's experience though you may not have faced it yourself), people would likely develop the maturity, sensitivity and selflessness necessary to love a husband or wife.

Empathy is Easier to Do Than Love

It's often said that love conquers all. The idea is credited to the classic Roman poet Virgil who in *The Eclogues* wrote, "Love conquers all things, so we, too, shall yield to love." The Bible in 1 Corinthians 13 references love as the greatest of all spiritual gifts. The Scripture continues:

> "Love is patient, love is kind. It does not envy, it does not boast, it is not proud. It does not dishonor others, it is not self-seeking, it is not easily angered, it keeps no record of wrongs. Love does not delight in evil but rejoices with the truth. It always protects, always trusts, always hopes, always perseveres."

This sounds fantastic, but the human biology and psychology that explain why people have difficulty achieving this and often act out of control when in love wasn't understood when this was written as it is today. It is now understood that love can involve elements such as emotion, attachment, and sexual drive that can wreck you if you're not ready for the ride. Biological anthropologist Helen Fisher, who has done extensive research on romantic love, says there are three brain systems: sex drive, romantic love, and attachment. Sex drive makes us want to spread our genes. Romantic love helps us to focus on one mate, while attachment helps us to bond with a person to raise children with. In a popular TED Talk called "Why We Love, Why We Cheat," Fisher said that romantic love is more than an emotion, but a drive that is even more powerful than the sex drive.

Fisher says that because of these different systems driving us, and releasing intense doses of dopamine in the brain, people are capable of loving different people at the same time. This is why some spouses may cheat on their marriage partner.

"It's as if there's a committee meeting going on inside your head as you try to decide what to do," Fisher said. "I don't think honestly that we're an animal that was built to be happy—we're an animal that was built to reproduce. I think the happiness we find, we make."

I believe it is very difficult for any person to truly love in a monogamous marriage without divine intervention. This singular deep love is about being able to hold the three types of love together in a monogamous relationship. You want to feel sex drive, romance and attachment to one person, right? It requires sacrifice in the way Scriptures describe. This love requires humans to tap deep into their spiritual life force, which I believe is God. This is why Christians and other faiths proclaim that God is love and that there is no greater love than one who would "lay down his life for a friend." This spiritual force is what holds the three loves together. The challenge with relying on what we humans typically *think* is love in a relationship is that we are often NOT tapping into God. Instead, we are tapping into our emotions only. We are talking about those physical goose bumps we feel when our "person of interest" is around or when we think of the person. We are responding to our passions, desires, and even lusts. This is one of the reasons why married couples become frustrated with each other. The emotions typically raise expectations that won't ever be satisfied. Meanwhile, true love is unconditional and absent of faulty expectations. Emotions are unreliable for sustaining a marriage—especially at the beginning of the relationship when the diapers are still on. We all know that a baby's diaper needs to be monitored often!

The challenge with emotions is that they are not intended for decision-making. You should never make a decision based on your emotions. My personal belief is that the purpose of emotions is to alert you that there is something important that is requiring you to take reasoned appropriate action. It's like an internal alarm that alerts you that a problem exists and/or motivates you to make a move. Do you see the pattern of the root "mo" in these words—e**mo**tion, **mo**tivate and **mo**ve? Once your "mo" is awakened, you need to assess the problem before you act. People who act first without assessing the situation usually create *mo'* problems. Decisions, particularly major decisions, should be made based on your mind and your gut only. Your mind or intellect assesses the problem and the pros and cons of the options for appropriate action. Your gut instinct is the final stopgap that taps into the spiritual realm, where I believe trusting God will result in the best outcome. Many of us can attest to times when we've properly assessed a situation, but failed to trust our guts. We feel the uneasiness and angst in our stomachs. We hear the still, assertive voice saying, "Don't say that. Do this instead." But we don't listen because our emotions say otherwise. So we end up making an emotional decision that causes even *mo'* headaches.

Empathy, on the other hand, doesn't trigger the emotional roller coaster that is often embedded in false love. Empathy relies more on intellect. It plays out in your brain, not your heart. Because most of us are immature when it comes to true love, empathy is easier to rely on because it doesn't cloud our vision with emotions. Essentially, empathy is the decision-making part of the "love conquers all process," without all of the emotional baggage. If a situation arises, and you can cut to the chase and focus solely on being empathetic, you're likely to have a much better outcome.

Empathy taps into your ability to care for another person. You connect them to your own experiences. The more you practice empathy, the more you develop the maturity that eventually grows your ability to tap into true love. Scientific brain research actually backs this up! Like strengthening your biceps by lifting weights in a gym, the more you engage in empathy, the stronger your ability to be empathetic becomes. Research shows that when you exercise the parts of the brain that are connected to positive emotions, that area of the brain actually begins to grow more synapsis. Blood flow increases to the area. You actually rewire your brain. Meanwhile, the area of the brain most connected with negative behavior diminishes in activity. The more you practice empathy, the more natural it will come to you. Eventually, your maturity strengthens your ability to tap into the highest level of empathy, which is true godly love!

Unfortunately, empathy is probably lacking in many of today's marriages because individuals are likely too focused on their own agendas and expectations tied to their old luggage. A case in point is a friend of mine from graduate school who lost his mother to complications from diabetes. It was a long, painful process for him to watch his mother wither away. Both of her legs had to be removed. She went blind.

Throughout the years, my friend's wife did not get along well with his mother. Both women had plenty of petty blame to own. The mother lived with the couple for a few years as she got sicker. She would often criticize the wife. She would complain about how the wife was rearing her grandchildren or that the wife should cook more for her husband, even though the wife also worked outside of the home. The wife would constantly remind the mother that there was a reason that her husband (the mother's ex-spouse) had divorced her decades ago. Fortunately, they eventually managed to bury much of their differences prior to the mother's death. My friend's wife was supportive during his mom's final years spent in a wheelchair in a nursing home, and his wife was by his side during the painful funeral. Still, she and his mother had caused much stress and frustration for my friend over the years. It took a toll on him.

Mother's Day came two months after my friend buried his mom. On that day, his sadness was deep and profound. He knew the day was coming, but didn't anticipate the degree of his emotions. However, he kept them under wraps because he did not want to spoil his wife's Mother's Day celebration. He was being empathetic toward her. He bought her a fabulous bouquet, a large card that the children signed, and also a personal "To My Dear Wife" card. He and the children planned maximum relaxation at a spa for her that would end with a delicious catered dinner.

That morning before attending church, my friend received a text message. Looking at his smartphone, my friend smiled. His wife was observing him in the same room just a few steps away. He responded to the text and then put his smartphone back into his breast pocket, as he normally would. His wife flipped her wig.

"Who was that from?" she asked intensely.

"What do you mean?" my friend responded with a calm surprise.

"You know what I mean. That text. That text message. Why in the hell is someone texting you like that on Mother's Day?"

My friend stared at his wife. His emotions rose from his toes, filled his eyes, and rushed to his brain. He blew a gasket.

"What in the hell is wrong with you? This text was from my friend Raven. We went to college together, remember? You know her, remember? You met her, remember? Didn't you insist on knowing or at least meeting *all* of my damn female friends? Raven is like a sister to me. She lost her mother to diabetes, too. You know this, remember? You signed the sympathy card, remember? Today is my first Mother's Day without my mom and all you can think about is who is texting me and what I might be doing with them? What's your damn problem?"

The room fell silent. My friend stormed out of the house to get away and took the family dog for a walk.

What would have defused this situation? Empathy. The wife should have realized that her husband was wounded. He was down. It was his first Mother's Day without the woman who had loved and nurtured him into becoming a man worthy of being called "husband." If she didn't have the words to console him, she could've done a Google search on the Internet for "words of comfort on Mother's Day." But she was too caught up in her own immature emotions and agenda to use some common sense.

Love *can* conquer all; however, the emotions of false love usually get the best of us. Love is sacrificial. It means, "I lay my agenda, my feelings, my life aside for your benefit and I expect nothing in return. I do this consistently no matter what the situation is. I yield to you. I submit to you!" Who in a relationship or marriage can honestly say that they are willing to go to this extent consistently for another person? Empathy is much more reliable and obtainable for most of us who are too immature to tap into God to be sacrificial.

If you focus intellectually on how you would feel if your partner or spouse was to take the action that you are considering doing, you might make a better decision. You might obey your gut. So if your spiritual muscles aren't strong enough yet, focus on empathy first. Apply empathy often. Eventually, empathy will bring out the capacity to overcome your fickle emotions. With practice you will mature, and the love force that is deep within you will flow because you are human and connected to God's Spirit.

RECAP

Set aside for a moment the notion that "love conquers all." In most marriages, the conqueror is empathy, the ability to identify with and feel another person's experience though you may not have faced it yourself. Empathy, unlike the false "pop-culture" emotional love that people are actually referring to, is intellect driven. It doesn't cloud your vision with emotions from the heart. Essentially, empathy is the decision-making part of the "love conquers all process," without all of the emotional baggage. It's also essentially the Golden Rule: Treat others the way that you want to be treated. A marriage imbued with empathy is more likely to be rooted in honesty. It has a greater chance of growing into a true deep love relationship that lasts. The type that is celestial, spiritual—a unified out of body experience.

CHAPTER 7

HOW TO PREPARE FOR MARRIAGE IN THE DIVORCE AGE:

Becoming an Automatic Parent and Still Finding Success in Marriage

On my radio show, I have done a series of premarital advice segments. They were a hit with the audience. I had expert psychologists, researchers and counselors on marriage and allowed listeners to call in and share their own experiences. Listeners particularly liked that the series was about lifting up the institution of marriage through sharing openly and honestly.

I received several e-mail responses. One particular e-mail expressed appreciation for a five-minute editorial I offered up that detailed my annoyance that Father's Day has become a day where deadbeat dads get more attention (though negative, it's still attention) than dedicated dads. The passionate e-mail from a stepdad epitomized the type of dads who deserve high praise. Many times it is the stepdad who is filling the gap that was created by the deadbeat. The e-mail, which follows, shows that blended families have succeeded for generations, and it expresses what it takes for them to succeed. I edited out names to protect the person's privacy:

Mr. LaVeist,

I appreciate your concern regarding using Father's Day to grandstand on deadbeat fathers. For a while, I stopped attending church on Father's Day because that was happening every year.

Thank you for acknowledging stepparents—specifically, stepfathers—on your radio show.

I am the second generation of a blended family. My grandfather migrated from North Carolina to Ohio in the Great "Field to Factory" migration to the North during the 1930s. Upon his arrival, he met and married my grandmother. He was widowed with five children, and she was widowed with five children. Together, they produced six children, my mother being the youngest. According to the stories that are so reverently told of my grandfather, he loved and treated my aunt and uncles as his own.

Fast forward to 1970; my mother met and married my stepdad. I was 6 years old at the time, and my younger brother was 2 years old. Our stepdad treated us as his own. I will, hereafter, refer to him as my dad. He nurtured us and taught us those things that men teach their sons. I learned to cook from my dad. I learned to change tires, engine oil, cut grass, and how to treat a wife from my dad. Through behavioral instruction, he also taught me how to be a stepparent. My dad was with my mom when she departed this earth in 1992; however, my bond with him wasn't dependent on his relationship with my mom. Actually, our relationship grew stronger after my mom died. My dad died in 2002, and although I have a relationship with my biological father, the death of my dad left me parentless.

In 1986, just shy of my 22nd birthday, I became a stepparent when I married a woman *who had two young daughters from a previous marriage. These little ladies, aged 7 and 5 years old at the time, decided to call me Daddy, although they knew their biological father. Over the next 28 years, I bonded with them through the loss of baby teeth (which I pulled), adolescent strife, injuries, "coming of age" issues, the birth of babies (my grandchildren), and all the things that are inherent to being a parent. Those two ladies are now 35 and 33 years old. Their mother and I are divorced; however, I am still Dad (Daddy when they need something). I hurt when they hurt, as I do with my three biological children.*

Throughout these relationships, no one refers to one another as "step" dad, daughter, or son. I have never heard the word "step" used in describing my grandfather or each other. Nor have I heard my dad refer to me as his stepson. I recall him always calling me or introducing me as his son. The only time I use "step" to describe my relationship with my daughters is when people try to figure out why they are only 15 and 17 years my junior.

We should call Mother's and Father's Days "Mom" and "Dad" Days, respectively. Those monikers speak to the true meaning of parenthood. Not every mother is a mom, nor every father a dad. I can just say that in my life, I'm the descendant of two great men who showed me that nurturing a child doesn't have to be confined to one with your DNA.

In this age of high divorce rate, chances are for many people that when they marry, they'll immediately become a parent, if they aren't one already. This is because of the high rates of divorce with children involved and the high number of children born out of wedlock. A 2011 Pew Research report estimated 42 percent of American adults (about 95.5 million people) have a "step relationship"—stepparent, stepchild, or step-grandparent. Divorce rates in blended or stepfamilies are nearly 70 percent. The top reasons why blended families split are over money and the rearing of the children. Issues with noncustodial parents—baby mommas and baby daddies—add to the blended family stress.

This being the reality, it's critical that you understand that blending a family is a balancing act that has to be accomplished with extreme care. Winning over your spouse's children is not a task that is to be taken lightly. It's unlikely that you can just charm or buy your way into this. Should you be more of a parent or should you be more of a friend to your stepchild? When do you apply tough love and when do you apply more of a listening, compassionate ear? Most of all, dealing with a blended family involves a fair amount of compromise to do whatever it takes that is best for the overall family and your "partnership of one." Perhaps your significant other is the one with the children, or perhaps you have children of your own, too, and your brood is about to grow, like in the classic 1970s TV sitcom, *The Brady Bunch*, where the remarried mom and dad each brought three children to their union. Whichever scenario applies to you, there are some things to keep in mind.

In a blended family, you will need specific tools to deal with the situation before the marriage. In any family, parents must be on the same page when it comes to childrearing styles and issues, but this is particularly important in a blended family because of the extra-complex dynamics. Rearing children is never a problem-free venture, particularly when you're fully engaged with them as a parent. However, knowing upfront what you are clearly getting yourself into—especially in a blended family situation—can help you to be prepared and to avoid a lot more heartache.

Come along and learn from one "automatic" parent's experience.

"She Ain't My Mother."

At a cocktail party, I got into a deep conversation with a woman I had just met. I wasn't surprised because when people put down a few drinks and feel relaxed among other interesting people, they typically open up about burning issues on their mind. They *really* tend to open up when they learn I'm a talk radio host. They want feedback and probably figure that I must be a good listener. I get this a lot when people are surprised to learn that I have adult children. This particular woman began sharing her story about how she is married to a great man whom she loves dearly, but has a teen daughter who is apparently a demon child. The woman was catching hell from her stepdaughter, but couldn't understand why. She thought the fact that she had "womaned up" for her stepdaughter when her biological mother hadn't should have brought appreciation and made her life heavenly.

"This young lady has such great potential," she said. "I can see her as a lawyer or architect or whatever she wants to be, but she just keeps sabotaging herself. Her grades are terrible, and she's always lashing out at me."

The woman said that her husband is equally frustrated with how his teen daughter treats his wife. He's gotten into many shouting matches with his daughter because he can see that his wife has been sweet to her. One day the woman took her stepdaughter shopping at the mall for school clothes. The woman allowed her stepdaughter to pick whatever clothes she wanted as long as they were presentable for school. She chose dresses, skirts and blouses and also got shoes and sneakers. Afterward, she and her stepmom had lunch and actually had a good time. During the drive home, the stepdaughter texted on her smartphone and listened to music with earphones on, but this was normal teen stuff. When they arrived home, the girl raced inside, and greeted her father with, "Hey, Dad!" on the way to heading up to her room. Her father stopped her.

"Hey, Baby. I haven't seen you all day. What did you get from the store?"

"Oh, just a little of this and that. No big deal," the daughter said.

"No big deal? Looks like you got a lot of bags there. Your stepmom spent a lot of money," he said, smiling adoringly at his wife while helping her carry the bags.

"So!" the daughter responded, while rolling her eyes.

"So? So? Did you at least tell your stepmother, 'Thank you'?"

"For what?" the daughter responded sharply. "Because she bought me something?"

Well, at this point, the father's blood pressure could be seen boiling his eyeballs to red. As if in slow motion, he reached back, his chest heaved, and then he began to move toward his daughter. Meanwhile, his wife moved in between them.

"It's OK, Honey," she said to her husband, putting her hands on his chest.

"The hell it is," he said. Then he turned to his daughter. "What kind of way is that for you to treat your stepmother who is doing nothing but her best for you?"

"She AIN'T my mother," the daughter yelled, and stormed into her room.

At the cocktail party, the woman, with tears welling in her eyes as she told the story, admitted that she was beside herself emotionally over her stepdaughter. She couldn't figure out how to get through to the girl.

Basically, there isn't much to figure out. The girl is not so much angry at her stepmother, but angry that her birth mother is NOT more like her stepmother. The birth mother has a drug problem, which has landed her in and out of rehab. This is the root of the marriage breakup with the girl's father. The teen's pain is that she wants her own mother to be more like her stepmother.

Oftentimes in a blended family situation, doing the right thing when it comes to your stepchild can cause even more problems than if you acted like a jerk. The more the stepparent's behavior upstages the child's image of the birth parent, the angrier the child can become. Of course, this is not always the case. There are many stepparent/stepchild relationships that work well—even better than biological relationships. But when this type of tension exists, the problem is typically emanating from the child's mind. The child will not likely understand that this is happening, but because of their immaturity level, they won't care about the pain they're causing the people who love them and are sacrificing for them. They are in pain, so they merely want to lash out to escape that pain.

Of course, good quality family counseling would best help such a situation. And it should happen before you get married. All members of the potential family, including the child or children, should be involved in the counseling together. After you're married, the most important thing necessary to ride this out is for the married couple to be unified and to not undermine each other. Stay on the same page about what are acceptable standards of behavior. Eventually, hopefully, the child will come around.

Another issue with blended families is how children should refer to the stepmom or stepdad in the first place. If you're "old school" like me, you believe that minors should refer to all elders with titles of respect such as Mr. or Ms. If you're like me and you believe that all of the children under your roof (biological or otherwise) should be treated with the same standard, then you will not use the word "step" when referring to any of your children. You'll insist that your stepchildren refer to you in the same way that your biological children will or do—Mom or Dad, as the letter at the beginning of this chapter states. Another possible alternative term is "bonus parent," for children who maintain strong ties to their noncustodial parent. But this does not necessarily work for every situation. Flexibility and compromise are keys.

A male friend of mine who is "old school," too, made such a compromise. He and his second wife each brought two children to their marriage. She brought two teen boys, and he brought two adolescent girls. The couple sat down before getting married to map out a strategy of how their children should refer to them. They purchased books on the topic of blended families and talked with family counselors. They weighed the pros and cons of having children refer to them by their first names or by titles such as Mom and Dad.

"I'm really, really not into having kids call me by my first name," my friend said. "But after doing the research and talking it over carefully with my wife—and us talking individually with our children—we concluded that being on a first-name basis was the best way to go for our particular family situation."

Meanwhile, my friend's soon-to-be wife didn't feel strongly either way regarding being called by her first name. The children wanted to use first names because of the relationships that they maintained with their noncustodial biological parents. The children were concerned about feeling as though they were being forced to choose between one parent and the other. They didn't want to feel disloyal to the parent they were not living with by referring to their stepparent as Mom or Dad. My friend told me that he didn't quite understand why the children were feeling as though they were "choosing" between parents. However, again, he compromised FOR THEM. He put his pride aside and did what he felt was best for the family.

Regardless of what decision you make, being on the same page with your spouse is crucial. The spouse of the biological children has to be willing to step in and translate and explain things about the stepparent to their children. Instead of overlooking disrespectful behavior, they have to be willing to step up and nip problems in the bud. Likewise, the stepparent has to be unlike a bull in a china shop, but rather a lamb to the slaughter if that's what it takes to help the child to adjust. You have to be able to play it cool when necessary, but also stand up for what's right at all times. How you stand up will need to change depending on the situation, though. Your motive shouldn't be about your own best interest and feelings, but to stand up for the best interest of the family and the child first. After all, YOU ARE the parent—the adult—and the child is still a child, even if they are a demon child for now, that is. Eventually, the stepchild will mature and step up . . . or grow older and step out on their own. Whether they are your biological child or not, if you are called to be their parent, you want to play your role well to help them to be successful.

RECAP

In this age of high divorce rate, it's quite likely that you will marry someone who already has children and/or that you may be bringing children into the marriage. There are unique considerations that men and women embarking on creating blended families need to take into account as they plan to head to the altar. Before you marry, you need to be in agreement on key factors concerning the children: what they'll call their stepparent (or perhaps better yet, "bonus parent"), and what will be considered acceptable behavior toward a stepparent are but a few.

CHAPTER 8

PRE-MARITAL DIVORCE ADVICE

My Dear Daughter,

Now that you are in your mid-20s, I'm sure that some things from your childhood are starting to bubble up to your consciousness. Some of it makes sense, but a lot is confusing. As you've begun finding your way in the world, I'm glad to hear that you have been reading various religious books and exploring different philosophies. I'm sure that there are Bible passages that have left you scratching your head. That's how it was for me particularly after I graduated from college and began to seriously ponder my life's purpose. I recall a passage that I read back in my mid-20s that disturbed the heck out of me. It raised a lot of questions. The story is about Jephthah and his daughter in the book of Judges, Chapters 11 to 12. Jephthah was a great warrior who judged over Israel for six years. But he had some serious unresolved "mommy and daddy issues." His mother was a prostitute. His half-brothers drove him away from home. Clearly this hurt him. Despite the rejection from his so co-called loved ones, Jephthah made a life for himself in a nearby town. He gained friends who followed him. He found acceptance and love.

Jephthah had one child, a daughter. You can tell from the Scriptures that she was a "daddy's girl" like you. You'll notice that it's just father and daughter—the two of them. Of course this raises questions. What happened between her dad and mom? What is the underlying mother/daughter story? Did she abandoned her daughter? Another puzzling thing is that the Bible clearly says that Jephthah loved his daughter, but the Bible doesn't provide her name, her identity. Why? The elders of the town came to Jephthah and asked him to lead a battle against their enemy. Reading in between the lines, you can tell that Jephthah was still hurt and vengeful that his people had cast him away. Now they were coming to him for help. He made them grovel. Jephthah told them that he would only lead the battle if they crowned him chief. They agreed.

Before going out to battle, Jephthah was understandably nervous. He prayed and swore an oath to offer a sacrificial offering to God if given the victory. It is recorded in Judges 11:31:

"Whatever comes out from the doors of my house to meet me when I return in peace from the Ammonites, shall be the Lord's, and I will offer it up for a burnt offering."

After winning the battle, which no doubt also heaped pain, and death upon many innocent women and children, Jephthah returned home. He was emotionally and physically spent. He was thinking of how wonderful it would be back *at home with his precious daughter—his blessing from God. I visualized his daughter home on her knees praying hard for her father's safe return from war. When she heard him coming, and saw him off in the distance, she raced out of the front door yelling, "Daddy, Daddy, Daddy . . . " and jumped into his arms, hugging him. Jephthah saw his beautiful daughter—his baby girl. He smiled broadly and his stress melted. But then his smile turned to horrific sorrow. He remembered his rash oath to God. He wailed as he placed his daughter on her feet to the ground and backed away. He fell to his knees and tore his clothes in agony.*

Even as a young man in my twenties, I felt Jephthah's pain as I read this. It messed with my head. I searched for meaning in the commentaries written by biblical scholars. The explanations either centered on Jephthah being foolish for making the oath or debates over whether the burnt offering was truly a human sacrifice. I couldn't understand why if God was so loving and just, and had approved of Jephthah's war, how could God allow his innocent daughter to suffer death over something that she obviously had nothing to do with? "What kind of God is this," I thought.

Well, when I was home alone and opened that envelope to read our paternity result, this story came to mind after my head finally cleared. I began to understand. It is about what the scholars say, but it is also a story about the inevitable consequences of unresolved pain. It is a story about how knowingly and unknowingly parents too often pass down their own pain to their children to suffer. It is a story about how those children become adults who will continue the chain of pain if they fail to confront their issues and heal. It is a story about how the innocent too often suffer for the guilty.

Yet, it is still a story of hope and victory. In the end, Jephthah's daughter displays great courage and faith. She is also a warrior, but for peace and love. You see, Daughter, where we encounter great pain, we can also find our greater hope—like Jesus Christ, who no longer hangs on a painful cross, but lives and brings peace. Great things are ahead for you, Daughter. I bless you with hope and constant peace all the days of your wonderful life.

Was I disappointed that I would not keep my marriage vows? Yes, initially, but certainly not shocked. What jolted me to my knees was the revelation that I mentioned at the beginning of this book: That during my divorce process, I learned after 21 years that my now-adult daughter is not my biological child.

My daughter's sudden and puzzling medical condition was the main catalyst that eventually led to the paternity test, but there were other stunning secrets that came to light, too. Out of respect for the privacy of each of my adult children, I will not delve into those additional hurtful details that they already know. However, I will share what happened that painful day that the envelope with the DNA results arrived in the mail at my home. Why expose any intimate details? I believe that our personal stories do not necessarily belong to us to keep locked up in our mental vaults. We are allowed, perhaps even chosen, to endure certain experiences so that others might learn from us or be helped by our testimonies. I can't go into the past and change what has already happened. Even the moment that occurred just five seconds ago cannot be changed! However, the past is ALWAYS present. It constantly makes us who we are. I accept what happens as it is, but simultaneously I dictate what will be. Therefore, NOW is always the best time to make a good decision that leads to our best *todays* and even better *tomorrows*.

It is my sincere hope that by experiencing my pain, a potential mother and father might become wiser in their decision making, particularly concerning sex and its likely effect on their innocent children. Someone has to stand up for and be responsible to the innocent child who could be the result of a selfish act. The world is full of adults who are actually *wounded children* because, in large part, their parents were selfish. These *hurt people* grow up and enter into marriages in which they in turn *hurt people*.

Some research estimates indicate that 30 percent of men in the United States who are paying child support may be victims of paternity fraud. Unknown numbers of men are raising children that are not biologically theirs. Some of them are understandably afraid to know the truth or are ashamed to reveal their stories. Not me. I love my daughter and could not have asked for a better one. Though we bear the pain of what was done to us, the burden of shame is neither mine nor hers to carry. Perhaps through my pain, YOU or someone who may be struggling silently with this issue (or another deep, painful secret) would stop feeling ashamed. If not, you could transfer your unresolved pain onto the ones whom you claim to love the most—like your innocent child; that child may someday become a wounded adult who will continue the chain of pain. Perhaps that child, that daughter, is you.

Tears for My Daughter

It was a Tuesday after a holiday weekend. The DNA results were actually supposed to arrive the previous Friday. I had been out of town visiting with friends and had a great weekend. Perhaps I needed that time of joy to prepare for the pain to come. When I pulled the envelope from the mailbox, I felt in my gut that the news would not be good. I sat at my kitchen table and stared at the envelope in my palms. I took a deep breath and then I prayed. I asked, "God, in the name of Jesus, please grant me the ability to handle these results if they are bad."

I slowly opened the envelope and slowly unfolded the document. Carefully, I read the words and numbers from top to bottom. Finally, I saw it: "Probability of Paternity 0%."

I began to hyperventilate. I dropped the document on the table as I stood abruptly. I paused and then paced toward my bedroom. Then I reversed and headed back to the table and then to the kitchen. I couldn't breathe. I couldn't think. My son who is asthmatic pierced my mind. After several years of rushing him to the hospital, for the first time I understood what it was like for him to have an attack. I headed to the front door and pulled the knob.

I need air. I need air. This can't be. I need air . . . I felt myself thinking as my heart raced.

I dashed outside and down the stairs, still trying to catch my breath. I began to walk and walk and walk . . .

I need air. This can't be. I need air. This can't be . . . I kept thinking. To passersby I must have looked either crazy or as if I were talking on my cell phone with an earpiece.

My feet and legs and arms kept moving. Down the sidewalk, street scenes and sounds went unnoticed. I felt completely alone.

I need air. This can't be. I need air. This can't be . . . I kept thinking.

I need air. This can't be. I need air . . .

Then, suddenly piercing through my mind, I heard clearly:

"Do you remember the day your daughter was born and that moment that you thought you saw a *glow* around her? You told everyone willing to listen that you saw love that day, didn't you? You've been telling her about that moment ever since, right? You never understood what that was about, right? Well, now you know."

My heart rate slowed some. My thoughts were pierced again:

"Do you remember how one of your friends at the gathering this past weekend spoke so lovingly about her father? Her random praise of her dad warmed your heart just as your mind drifted to thoughts of this DNA test, right? Well, your daughter talks about you in that way to her friends all of the time, too. She is going to continue to brag about YOU—her daddy."

I felt my breath returning slowly. I began to realize where I was. I thought of a family member who had a wrenching experience with his first adoptive child that broke his heart, yet he had the courage to adopt a second time.

"His pain will be your gain. Look at the love and commitment that their family has. You will be courageous like him, too."

Finally, I stopped walking. I cupped my face with my palms and took deep breaths.

In my thoughts I heard again:

"Now didn't you already decide what you would do if the

DNA results were bad?"

I began walking back to my apartment. I replayed the plan over in my mind. *Call the attorney and tell him what's going on,* I thought.

When I'd dashed out of my apartment, I'd left my keys and smartphone on the kitchen table. I picked up the smartphone and punched buttons. I found the name of the attorney I had come to know from our work with the same community organization. I had already decided that he would be the one to call. I left a message with his assistant. He was wrapping up another call and would get back to me within five minutes. When he did, I told him about the DNA test results. He was shocked.

"Are you OK? Man, I'm sorry this happened to you," he said. "If the annulment laws were not so antiquated, this would be an open and shut case."

Then he asked, "You're getting divorced? LaVeist, why didn't you call me sooner?"

I just grabbed my forehead as I held the phone silently to my ear.

"OK. OK. There is still time to have a judge to reopen and challenge the current divorce proceeding filed by your wife," he said. "Don't worry. I'll get on it. You are going to be OK. Your daughter is going to be OK."

As I ended the call, it hit me: Would my daughter *really* be OK? I began to think about the lifelong impact this would have on her. Being a 21-year-old woman who is trying to figure out her place in the world is difficult enough. Imagine learning that the man you had known as "Daddy" your entire life is NOT your biological father? Imagine realizing that your own mother had done this to you. Imagine standing in the bathroom, looking in the mirror, and through your tears wondering, "Who am I?"

It was too much for me. In my bedroom, I began to wail. I fell to my knees.

"God, you've got to protect my daughter, please!" I screamed through my tears.

"Please, Jesus, take care of her, please!"

My chest tightened. I felt as though I was going to vomit.

Then suddenly, in my thoughts, I heard:

"OK, enough. Get up now. It's done!"

A calm began to come over me. I went to the bathroom. I washed and dried my face.

I walked to my home office and sat behind my computer to work.

The thoughts continued to break my concentration, though.

How am I going to tell her?
Will she continue to love me, or will she reject me?
Will I change or continue to love her always?
Oh, God, our relationship will never be the same.

Several hours later, I heard a key in the front door lock. My daughter was returning home from a day of college classes and work.

I heard her precious voice.

"Hey, Daddy!" she called to me as she walked to my desk, hugged me, and kissed me on the cheek.

My heart warmed the same way it always had. Like when she was a little girl and I'd come home from a long day's work. When she would dash to the front door and hug my knee. Like when I'd hold her hand as we took father-daughter trips to the corner store. I would break my own rules against eating candy and fill her pockets. Like when she would sing to me the song, "You Are So Beautiful" and I would grin. And her voice warms me still as I write this passage more than a year later, listening to her laugh while talking on her smartphone in her bedroom across the hall.

I Was Only "Technically" Married

As I stated previously, I believe most divorces start BEFORE the marriages even happen. People ignore signs that they shouldn't get married in the first place. However, a marriage can start off free of warning signs and even be euphoric for years. People can change or grow apart along the way. This is why it is good to understand how you might part if it becomes inevitable. So, no, a prenuptial agreement isn't a bad idea. Prenups outline how you will retain the assets you brought into the marriage or divvy up what you acquire together. Personally, I doubt that I would require a prenup, unless, perhaps, I had significant financial assets that require protection. I would not be against signing one for similar reasons. Agreeing to a prenup doesn't necessarily mean you're planning for a divorce. It could mean you're being proactive in potentially avoiding a tremendous amount of stress and strife later.

Divorce is often emotionally and financially costly. You could spend up to about $1,000 or more in attorney and court fees if the two of you *can* agree to part amicably. If you can't agree, those costs could be $10,000 or much more for a trial. Depending on the state you live in or file in, a divorce could take at least one year of living separately before you can file for it. It could take at least another year or more before the split is finalized. For some people the process has taken up to 10 years or more to be official. Some people remain married but legally separated because of financial or other reasons. An estimated 50 percent of marriages in the United States end in divorce. Divorces are often messy, and innocent children are typically the collateral damage. Perhaps if more couples analyzed the current state of their premarital love relationships more carefully and "played the videotape all the way out," there would be less drama and unhappy endings to their marriage movies.

Earlier, I mentioned that I realize now that all these years I had only been "technically" married. Therefore, it follows that I am also "technically" divorced. So on applications, I simply select "single." I say this because of my odyssey in the legal justice system during my divorce case. I now refer to the system as the "legal technicality system." I have the Hon. Judge Jerrauld C. Jones of the Norfolk Circuit Court to thank for educating me about this.

Jones was the judge who presided over my divorce proceeding and who issued the initial ruling against me. In spite of the facts and clear evidence presented by my attorney. In spite of Jones's initial agreement that I had proven adultery had occurred, Jones denied my petition for a divorce based on adultery.

Again, out of respect for my adult children, I will share some of the facts, but I will avoid rehashing all of the case's details here. They would be offended by much of the statements, facts, and behaviors by the players involved. *LaVeist v. LaVeist* is part of Virginia's public court record now. You can look up the case and request the transcripts, including documents from the Court of Appeals of Virginia and the Supreme Court of Virginia.

To avoid being railroaded if you have to get a divorce, you'll want to do the following:

- Make sure that you have a competent attorney from the start.
- Don't allow your emotions to sway you into trusting your spouse to do the right thing by you or your children.
- Make sure that your attorney is and has you thoroughly prepared for every possible outcome, especially the worst case scenario.
- Don't assume ANYTHING—especially that the judge (or jury) will render justice.

Earlier in my career as a reporter, I covered some court cases up close. I've reported on innocent people who were railroaded and criminals who got exactly what they deserved. Previously, being in court for a traffic ticket was about as personal as my experience had been before a judge. Trust me, no person should be subjected to what I experienced in divorce court.

Now for my odyssey in Judge Jones's court. I will try my best to deliver just the facts . . .

First, a little background about this man. Jones was a member of the Virginia House of Delegates from 1988-2002 while he was in private law practice. In published news reports, Jones, a Democrat, had expressed a strong desire to be a member of the U.S. House of Representatives. Jones pushed to get legalized gambling in Virginia, which has failed. He came in third in the 2001 race for lieutenant governor. To fill a vacancy, former Virginia Governor and current U.S. Sen. Mark Warner appointed Jones to the Norfolk Juvenile and Domestic Relations Court in 2005. He was then appointed to the Norfolk Circuit Court in 2008 by current U.S. Sen. Tim Kaine, who is also a former Virginia governor, also to fill a vacancy. Warner and Kaine are Democrats. You may remember that Kaine was the vice presidential running mate of Hillary Clinton, who lost the historic 2016 presidential election to Donald Trump, a Republican.

Both Warner and Kaine are known for being honorable men who have good judgement. I have interviewed Warner, including on my radio show. Warner is a good man. To both of them, Jones was likely a political appointment that made sense. Unfortunately in Virginia, voters don't elect judges. They are typically appointed by the General Assembly. Virginia and South Carolina are the only two states that continue to use the legislative election method. Legislators choose judges to serve on the state appellate and general jurisdiction courts (governors handle special appointments, such as filing vacancies). Other states have abandoned this method because the appointments become more about partisan politics and fail to lead to a fair and impartial judicial branch. Judges are more beholden to their political colleagues and former law school classmates than the everyday people (voters) of the state.

As a journalist in Virginia, I didn't cover Jones and never interviewed him. However, I was aware of him and recall an introduction once during a community event in Norfolk. My divorce case was originally assigned to a different judge. Standing in the somewhat crowded courtroom for the initial hearing, I was a little concerned for my family's privacy, particularly my daughter. There were a couple of people in the courtroom who knew me from my radio show. I talked briefly with one of them and she asked me about promoting her upcoming event. While we exchanged contact information, I heard the bailiff shout, "LaVeist versus LaVeist." He said the case would be heard by "Judge Jones" in a different courtroom. I was relieved.

My attorney and I stepped into the empty courtroom. Oddly, my case was the only one that had apparently been reassigned to Jones. When Jones walked in from his chambers, I recognized him. I thought, "Well, perhaps at least I'll get a fair hearing regardless of the outcome."

My first sign that things would not go well occurred more than a month later at a subsequent hearing. Jones refused to issue a "motion to compel" one of the alleged paramours that I subpoenaed as a witness. A motion to compel orders the uncooperative party to comply or face possible punishment, such as having to pay attorney fees. The alleged paramour was a no show for back-to-back scheduled hearings. At the time of this writing, this man, believe it or not, remains a Virginia state trooper and a pastor of a church. The second hearing that the trooper/preacher missed was specifically rescheduled to accommodate his work schedule. The delay cost me time and money in legal fees. Via e-mail, the opposing attorney revealed that he had talked to the trooper/preacher (even though the guy was my witness) and gave him advice. Jones was made aware of this. He was fine with it. Apparently Jones's priority was to not embarrass the trooper/preacher by sending a process server to the state police headquarters where he was stationed.

When the trooper/preacher finally testified while under oath to God, he stated that the defendant asked him to provide pastoral marriage counseling. They met ALONE in his home. Then they drove around town in his car to run errands, he said. Apparently I would've been the third wheel in these *pastoral counseling* sessions. Under intense questioning from my attorney, the trooper/preacher confirmed that he and the defendant had other *private sessions* too. He admitted that sexting occurred, but he denied being a paramour. The trooper/preacher contradicted the sworn deposition that my attorney took from him months prior. When my attorney would point out these contradictions, the trooper/preacher repeated, "I don't recall . . . I don't recall . . ." Jones responded by saying only that clearly "something inappropriate" had happened.

That was it.

The second sign of bad things to come occurred while I was on the witness stand. In questioning me about why I signed a separation agreement without consulting a lawyer, Jones asked about my education level. I have a master's degree and I was completing a doctorate. First I was puzzled by Jones's line of questioning. But then it became clear that Jones was *passing judgment on me* more than judging the facts of the case; since I wasn't forced to sign, I should live with the consequences of my actions. For example, Jones was unmoved by the fact that the defendant's previous attorney, who had prepared our separation agreement, had withdrawn from the case citing his "conflict of interest." The attorney bailed after learning of the paternity test results. I learned after that the law required that I be advised of my right to my own lawyer.

Anyone who has been through a divorce knows that it can be a highly emotional and volatile time. In my case, I had other personal matters that demanded attention—most notably my daughter's mysterious illness. This while also staying focused on finishing my doctorate and working a fulltime job. I was trying to keep the peace, while moving on with my life as soon as possible. Simply put, I let my emotions cloud my judgement. During a divorce, it is vital to strip out your emotions and make logical decisions. Any competent lawyer could have helped me do that. I made a big mistake by not hiring my own lawyer to handle the separation agreement. If I had known the hidden truth about my daughter and the adultery, I definitely would not have signed it. Apparently, Jones declined to wrap his head around how such an intelligent man could make such a mistake.

Sitting in Jones's courtroom, I observed him carefully for signs of what he might be thinking. I was not encouraged. For example, at the beginning of each hearing, Jones was cavalier when he swore us in under oath before God. It was just a mere formality to him. In other courtrooms, I've been impressed by how seriously many judges take this part of the proceeding, even over a traffic ticket. They pause. They make sure everyone is attentive. And they speak clearly and loudly, "Do you swear to tell the truth, the whole truth, and nothing but the truth, so help you God?" Not Jones. Each time he would fast-talk mumble his way through the oath.

Throughout the trial, Jones allowed the opposing attorney to be belligerent and disrespectful. The opposing attorney constantly objected and interrupted my attorney, who carried himself like a true Southern gentleman who respected the court. During one of the earlier hearings, the opposing attorney surprisingly referred to his own client as a "loose woman" in establishing his rebuttal to my argument. He said that I should have known what I was getting myself into when I decided to marry. The dictionary definition of "loose woman" is one who "commits adultery" or simply, "an adulteress." So hypothetically, even if Jones' wife, Judge Lyn Simmons, who sits on the Domestic Relations Courts bench in Norfolk, were to commit adultery, it would apparently be acceptable to call her a "loose woman" in court?

To the casual observer, Jones would appear to be personable and thoughtful. He is deceptive. Each day in court, Jones seemed less and less interested in my case—as if he had already made up his mind. A couple of times, he pulled his mobile phone from his pocket and began to thumb its keyboard. Initially, I thought that Jones was perhaps making a note to himself about the case. But during another moment, while my attorney was making another vital point, Jones abruptly pulled his phone out again. He was apparently texting someone.

Under questioning from my attorney, the defendant admitted under oath to committing adultery with a different paramour. Under questioning from my attorney, that paramour, a low level staff member at a university, admitted under oath that he and the defendant had sex at least five times during the marriage. Suddenly, Jones halted my attorney in mid-sentence. Jones said the following, which is taken directly from the court transcript:

> *"There seems to be concession, Counsel . . . that there has been now uncontroverted proof of adultery taking place during the marriage. And what he says is, that being the case that we don't need—we don't need any other evidence of adultery."*

At this point, my attorney stopped and began to wrap up the case.

However, when it came time for the ruling, Jones shocked us all. Jones ruled that I had not proved adultery. He said that I failed to establish a date and time. Instead, he granted the defendant a "no fault" divorce.

"What Do You Love Most About the Law?"

I've come to realize that some people are just intellectually slothful, judges included. Meanwhile other judges are scholars who truly love grappling with the law and seeking justice. For example, the late Antonin Scalia, the former associate justice of the Supreme Court of the United States, is not a judge whose rulings I often agreed with. However, I respected him. Watching him in interviews and based on his attentive approach to cases, I had no doubt that he loved the law.

One of my favorite movies, *Philadelphia*, which is about a lawyer who has HIV/AIDS, has in it a wonderful line about loving the law. The movie stars two of my favorite actors, Denzel

Washington and Tom Hanks. While on the witness stand, Hanks's character answers the question, "What do you love most about the law?" He responds:

" . . . that every now and again . . . not often, but occasionally . . . you get to be a part of . . . justice being done. That really is . . . quite a thrill when that happens."

Unfortunately, to others in the "legal technicality system," the court of law is just another place of employment. Or even worse, the bench is a perch from which they play god.

Obviously, I believe Jones's management of his courtroom and my case was literally, well, *criminal*. Since he did not issue an opinion, it is difficult to understand how he could on one hand agree with BOTH attorneys that the defendant committed adultery—that Virginia's marriage law had been broken—but then backtrack and say that I didn't establish the date and time, so adultery wasn't proved. How can this be? Well, I guess it's like what President Bill Clinton said during his grand jury testimony concerning his impeachment over his sexual relationship with Monica Lewinski:

> *"It depends upon what the meaning of the word 'is' is. If the—if he—if 'is' means is and never has been, that is not—that is one thing. If it means there is none that was a completely true statement."*

So, adultery IS not actually adultery even when the people involved in committing the adultery admit under oath that they committed adultery. Is this *really* the intent of the Virginia General Assembly? Is this the will of the people in any state?

The Appeals Court declined to overturn Jones's ruling, citing a "procedural default." It said that my attorney did not properly follow a certain citation rule in filing the appeal. Therefore, the court refused to review the transcript that I quoted here where Jones clearly stated that I *had* proven adultery. A little known disturbing fact about the Appeals Court is that many of the appeals are NOT decided by actual judges, but by law clerks. The Supreme Court of Virginia rejected my appeal, claiming that it lacked jurisdiction in the case. The court wrote no opinion (the court is not required to, though it should be). Again, none of these judges (nor clerks) have faced or will face a vote of the people of Virginia.

Update Antiquated Marriage Laws

One thing that I do not necessarily fault Jones for is his ruling against my petition to have my marriage annulled. The two-year statute of limitations had long passed. An annulment is when a marriage is undone as if the marriage never occurred. In most states, there are a limited number of reasons that can serve as grounds for an annulment. For example, if one of the people were minors. Another reason is paternity fraud.

Paternity fraud is primarily when a woman identifies or leads a man to believe that he is the biological father of a child when she knows that he is not or when she has a strong reason to believe that he is not. When a man and woman are married, the husband is presumed to be the father of every child born during the marriage. This dates back to English common laws during medieval times to prevent children from being labeled illegitimate and without rights. However, we are living in the information age of the 21st century. Artificial insemination and DNA testing are more common. Women have more equal rights and wage earning potential to provide for themselves. Ironically, in Britain, paternity fraud is correctly considered a criminal act punishable by fines and prison time. A few states in the United States consider it a crime as well.

If you commit fraud by writing bad checks and are caught, you will likely have to repay the victims and do prison time. But if a woman commits paternity fraud and is caught, the man she victimized will still likely have to pay child support and/or alimony for several years. Meanwhile, the child that the courts claim to be looking out for has little to no recourse either. To me, paternity fraud is an attack on a child's identity. Our DNA shapes our lives. Depending on the laws of a given state, the child cannot realistically sue her mother for damages or force her to reveal the biological father; the child cannot realistically sue the biological father either. It is high time that states, such as Virginia where I currently live, update their marriage and family laws to fit the realities of our current times.

I was not aware that paternity fraud was such a problem in the United States and worldwide until I began researching it. Firm statistics on the problem are difficult to nail down because many men are ashamed or don't know. Some studies indicate that one million husbands may be affected annually. Even men who have been able to prove they are not the biological fathers of children are often still forced by the "legal technicality system" to pay child support. Sadly, this injustice is likely very common among people in professions such as the military (which is dominant in Virginia), where spouses are often deployed for long stretches.

Paternity fraud obviously happens to married and unmarried heterosexual men. A wife can also be victimized by a husband who, prior to marrying, fails to disclose that he has a child by another woman. This too can be grounds for an annulment. Considering the use of artificial insemination or donor eggs and sperm, paternity fraud could technically happen to same-sex couples, too. The debate around paternity fraud and how to properly address it typically focuses on whether the father who has been wronged should still pay child support. The debate gets further muddied by the child support system's goal to sustain itself financially by getting tough on deadbeat dads. Simply put, the state doesn't want to foot the child support bill. The state is correct to seek provision for the innocent child who has also been wronged. But in doing so, the laws end up pitting the child and the "duped dad" against each other. Both the innocent man and the child get TOTALLY screwed. Meanwhile, the woman who has wronged both the man and her child is often TOTALLY let off the hook. It is the perfect crime! The laws should protect and provide redress for all of the people who have been wronged. The laws should place the burden of responsibility on the person(s) to whom it belongs: the mother and her paramour.

Making paternity fraud primarily about whether to pay or not to pay child support cheapens the issue and the devastating impact it has on two innocent human beings. For the child, to not know her true identity could cause psychological wounds that never heal. For the father, the feeling of betrayal and loss hurts deeply. Matters get even worse if the angry father rejects the innocent child, which is sadly often the case. As a society, we essentially make light of all of this with TV shows where the host proclaims, "You ARE (or) ARE NOT the father!" and sitcoms, movies and reality shows that popularize gold digger "baby mommas" and deadbeat "baby daddies." As a society, we can't realistically legislate morality, but we can certainly bring fairness to our laws to address wrongs that impose damage on others—particularly innocent children who often have to endure the pain well throughout their adult lives.

JUSTICE FOR MARRIED MEN

Part of the problem of why most paternity fraud laws are unjust is that they not only let the mother off the hook, but they lump together unmarried and married couples. My focus here is on married heterosexual men. Marriage is supposed to be special union of commitment. It brings with it particular important rights recognized by state and federal laws. This is why the struggle for marriage equality has been so important. As I said, paternity fraud is grounds for annulment. However, in most states the victimized spouse (typically the husband) must discover the offense within two years of the child's birth. This is the case in Virginia. If discovered in time, the offended spouse could then have up to five years to file for an annulment, depending on the state. Again, this is supposedly to protect the interest of the innocent child. But what about the special rights, responsibilities, burdens and benefits that come with marriage? If the offense is grounds for annulment, should it matter how long it took to uncover the fraud? If the fraud is grounds for annulment, then why should the person who committed the fraud STILL be eligible to receive not only child support payments, but the benefits of having been married? Benefits, such as property and asset distribution, alimony, and access to a former spouse's Social Security retirement? Is it just me who thinks this aspect of the "legal technicality system" is grossly unfair?

Welcome to my world.

Any time limit on whether a spouse can seek an annulment should begin at the point the paternity fraud is proved. Once the DNA test is in hand, the spouse should separate themselves immediately and have at least two years to file for an annulment. Some states realize they are behind the times and have adjusted their laws to some degree. For example, at the time of this writing, Maryland allows unlimited time to challenge paternity using DNA testing. In a few states there have been bills to make paternity fraud a criminal act punishable by a fine and prison time. Not in Virginia. Lawyers advised me that I could file a civil suit and possibly win a judgement from $1,000 to maybe $10,000 if lucky. It would cost at least $5,000 just to retain an attorney from the start. Do the math.

The scenario that rewards paternity fraud can be avoided by requiring every child born during a marriage to automatically be tested to establish paternity. It's a simple test. Just swab the mouths of the husband and child or match the fluid from the fetus (home DNA tests should not count and are not admissible in court). The test should be waived only if both spouses agree to forgo their right to know. Arguments against mandatory paternity tests typically hinge on testing being too expensive. Costs vary from as low as $30 to $500 depending on the type of test. The costs could probably be lower if done as part of other prenatal tests to check the health of the child while in utero. The cost could also be covered by health insurance. Some states, such as Arizona, pay the upfront cost of a paternity test requested by the alleged father. If the test is positive, the father is obligated to repay the state.

Some say that if the state mandates such a test, it would be an invasion of privacy and violation of civil rights. Couples are required to take tests for certain diseases before marriage. By law, husbands are automatically considered the legal father of children born during a marriage. Courts impose payments for child support and alimony. If paternity cannot be established and government welfare agencies have to pick up the bill, those costs to taxpayers will be much higher than the paternity test. Relinquishing some rights for the betterment of society is normal. We do it all of time, such as having to wear a seatbelt when driving a car. DNA tests have been used to free people who have spent years in prison for crimes they did not commit. Why shouldn't a paternity test help provide justice for a husband and a child that have been wronged by a wife and mother? Is it better that the states like Virginia essentially reward someone for committing an act that causes so much pain, especially to an innocent child who could grow up to become a wounded adult?

LEGISLATORS CAN IMPROVE THE LAW

I've never been one to bow easily when fighting for justice. This is one of the reasons why I became a journalist. So, I met separately with three Virginia legislators to share my story and request that they update the laws to address paternity fraud. My daughter attended one of the meetings. The legislators—two men and one woman—were visibly moved during the meetings. They each clearly saw the injustice. I stressed that at minimum, the law should allow the child to sue to learn their true genetic background, especially for medical reasons. The Virginia General Assembly is the nation's oldest continuous law-making body. It needs updating in many areas. However, I'm not naïve. It takes a lot to get legislation passed. Oftentimes politicians do not move on complex issues unless opinion polls favor them or if there is a strong financially backed lobby for change. I had prepared myself for nothing to be done.

Before the start of the 2017 session, one of the male legislators had his assistant respond to my follow up. She said that his list of bills to submit was full and that I should contact the legislator in my district. The other male legislator (who actually met me and my daughter together in his office) did not get back to me with a final decision at all. His silence was his answer. But then I received a call from the office of the female lawmaker. Her assistant told me that Senate Bill 1495 (SB 1495) had been submitted and that she would like me to testify before the Courts of Justice Committee. The bill would have removed the restriction against filing an annulment if the marriage was two years or older.

The majority of America's laws were and are written by men, many of whom are white and of socioeconomic privilege. They are also often paternalistic in their thinking. Many male lawmakers have ignored paternity fraud for fear of being accused of bashing women. Partly because she is a woman, but mainly because she is a deeper thinker, the legislator who introduced the bill knows that such an attitude is paternalistic nonsense. Too many lawmakers from the same cloth means blind spots are inevitable. When our legislative bodies have a more balanced mix of women and people of different racial, ethnic and socioeconomic backgrounds, it obviously increases the chances of getting laws on the books that best match the composition and will of the people.

Honestly, driving to the state capitol, I felt grateful that she introduced the bill, but I had very low expectations that the bill would survive the committee. Senate Room B was packed with many people present to speak for or against other bills. When called to the podium, I briefly shared my story. The audience hushed. Members of the committee visually seemed very concerned about what I said. They obviously saw the problem, but did they *understand* it? The committee chair asked if there was anyone present who opposed the bill. A man who said he represented an attorney's group and that he practiced family law came to the podium to voice opposition. He said that the two-year restriction has been standard for several years and that the law was written to protect children from being "bastards." He offered other objections that basically amounted to saying, the law has always been this way, so why change for one person (Translation: This bill will cut into the revenue of my family law practice). One committee member asked a question about bigamy (Huh?) and how this proposed change might apply. Another committee member expressed concern about the negative impact the annulment would have on the child. "Your daughter is older, but what if the child was 14 years old?" he said. I responded that an annulment is about the marriage—the fraudulent relationship between the man and woman. It would be no different for the child than if the parents got a divorce. It would also be no different for the child than if the parents were never married, but were co-parenting. The legislator looked at me with a puzzled expression. Apparently, he couldn't wrap his mind around this point.

In 2013, a judge in Chester, Virginia was faced with a similar scenario. For 13 years a man was led to believe that he was the biological father of a girl. Likewise, the girl believed that he was her biological father. The man and the girl's mother never married. The man became $23,000 in debt for child support, so the mother took him to court. The man had a paternity test done that revealed he is not the biological father, but according to the law he still had to pay child support because he signed the girl's birth certificate when she was born. According to published reports, the judge commented that there are "certain aspects of the law that seems grossly unfair." Instead of making the man pay $200 a month, the judge ordered him to pay $1 per month. At that rate, it would take 1,917 years to pay the $20,000 debt. Clearly this Virginia judge did not want to see the man punished because of an obvious flaw in the law. Clearly this judge issued a creative and just ruling because he "loves the law."

So, what would have been different for the daughter had the man and her mother been married? The only difference is that the mother (the person who committed the fraud) could have made out like a bandit. The mother would have been eligible for alimony and more in a divorce. Meanwhile, the daughter would be left with only the same painful and potentially broken relationship with a man that she had been calling "Dad" all of her life.

In the end, the SB 1495 vote was split, but the committee killed the bill saying, "too many potential unintended consequences." That's what politicians tend to do when challenged to think a little deeper. Outside in the hallway, I thanked the senator who introduced the bill. She too expected the same no vote. Virginia's lawmakers know for sure now that there are serious problems with the paternity fraud laws. There are several things that could be done, which I've outlined here. But because the issue isn't politically expedient, they won't do anything unless forced. Instead, lawmakers would rather craft bills that require people to pull their pants up in public, or that dictate which public restroom a person must use based on their birth certificate.

Like I stated previously, I expected the bill to be killed. Life is often not fair. My philosophy is that you simply fight hard and do the right thing as best you can so that you can look yourself in the mirror during the day and sleep in peace at night. Then, you wake up the next morning, smile and keep on movin' on. I did my part as a resident of the Commonwealth of Virginia. I will also continue to vote each Election Day. I'll be fine. My hope is that someone who might otherwise explode and do something tragic, will learn from my story, avoid the pitfalls, and or stay calm and find peace.

My advice to everyone in the United States is to stay as far away from the legal technicality system as you possibly can. Whatever you *think* the law is or should be, chances are it *is not*. I would like to believe that most judges, lawyers and even politicians desire to do the right thing, like the senator who introduced SB 1495. However, the system is not justice-driven, but rather money-driven. It is infested with self-servants who use the system to advance their own career agendas and who have convinced themselves that they are above the people.

And speaking of self-servants . . .

In spite of my head-scratching odyssey in Judge Jerrauld C. Jones's kangaroo courtroom, I continue to respect our legal system. It's the only one we've got. I still recommend going to court for justice rather than taking matters into your own hands. As a Christian, I believe that holy matrimony represents the relationship between Jesus Christ and his church. I realize now that God blessed my sincerity to do the right thing, particularly by my children, but God never blessed my marriage. The truth of my daughter's paternity was hidden from me, but not God. Confession and honesty is central to a relationship with Christ. A marriage built on anything otherwise could never reflect Christ and his church. This is simple logic to me. So, I believe, that in God's eyes, I was never under the covenant of holy matrimony.

Marriages are federally protected and are recognized across all 50 states, whereas civil unions are not. Both must be approved and registered by a state. In America, you can get married and divorced without ever setting foot in a church. However, by law you MUST first get a marriage license from a state government. To me, the law views marriages (including ceremonies in places of worship) as mere transactions between two willing parties. So if a circuit court judge shows you that your marriage is just a "legal technicality," believe it. My "legal technicality" began in a justice of the peace office in Las Vegas, Nevada, and ended in a courtroom in Norfolk, Virginia.

The next time I say "I do" will actually be my first holy marriage.

If You Must Divorce

Though it could be ideal for a marriage to endure forever "for better or for worse," oftentimes divorce *is* the better option. If children are present, they usually get wounded in the crossfire as the adults are often too caught up in their individual agendas. Separating peacefully, or at least quietly in the best interest of the children, is the best path, but often the path that is least followed. A key reason why people can't agree to separate peacefully is that they typically can't control their emotions after they realize the love has gone. A lawyer friend told me that this is a big and growing problem that she sees in his practice—a husband or wife or both who just can't keep their cool. What begins as civil soon turns into an "uncivil war."

I remember back in the 1980s watching the original version of the show *The People's Court*, which is probably the first reality TV show. Back then, *The People's Court* (which now stars Judge Marilyn Millan) starred Judge Joseph Wapner, who offered arbitration for small claims cases. The show spawned other court shows, including *Divorce Court*, which has become the longest running courtroom series. However, the tagline of *The People's Court*, "D*on't take* the law into your own hands: you *take* 'em to *court*" is advice that all divorcing couples should take to heart. As my lawyer friend said, people have a difficult time keeping their emotions in check. Getting emotionally riled over a spouse who you either no longer want to be with or who does not deserve you is a waste of valuable energy. You could be devoting that energy to your children's emotional needs and to getting yourself prepared for the next phase of your life. Instead of following your spouse around town, or stalking him or her online on social media, or confronting their lover by telephone, just take them to court and have them subpoenaed to testify.

A discovery deposition is a powerful tool to use to confront your cheating spouse or their lover(s), if you choose. The purpose of discovery is to get a sense of what the witness will say. It's about getting as much ammunition as possible to help your lawsuit. Lawyers like to have a good idea of how a witness will answer a question before putting them on the stand. The person subpoenaed has to testify—get this—under oath! That testimony can be brought up in court later during the trial. Though discovery typically happens in a lawyer's office, it is an official court proceeding. The court reporter swears in the witness who promises to give truthful testimony. Of course, people still lie at these hearings. However, doing so puts them at risk of perjury and possible prosecution, a fine, or jail time. But your chances of finding out the truth, or at least getting some satisfaction watching your spouse or their lover squirm, is priceless.

It's not easy to rationalize in this way and to keep your emotions in check during a divorce. Passions are aroused because at one point you obviously had strong, intimate feelings for your spouse. The ego can drive you to want to get even—to perhaps even want to do physical harm, including to yourself! However, that will only lead to more pain for the innocent victims, typically your children. If the marriage is dead, then the best thing to do is to negotiate a separation agreement and stay out of a drawn out, emotionally draining court proceeding. Have competent lawyers draw up the terms. Hire your own lawyer to look over the agreement for your best interest. Then go your separate ways in peace. A civil separation is ideal, but unfortunately, an "uncivil war" is more likely. If you can't come to terms, don't take the law into your own hands. You can get much more accomplished legally if you get a lawyer and *take 'em to court. In the end, the final cost will be well worth your peace of mind.*

Watch Out For the "He-Man Woman Haters"

Those of us who grew up on the old *Our Gang* or *The Little Rascals* TV series of the 1930s remember characters such as Spanky, Alfalfa and Buckwheat. One of the classic episodes was about the He-Man Woman Hater's Club, where the group of boys pledged to never show an interest in girls. Deep down, they are actually just afraid of being hurt. Well, the world is full of apparent "he-men" who are still hurt little boys who actually prey on wounded women. This is particularly the case involving recently divorced women.

Going through a divorce is like mourning a death because, in fact, the marriage has died. You will likely go through all of the stages of grief. The Kübler-Ross model lists five basic grief stages:

1. Denial — No, no, this can't be happening.
2. Anger — I can't believe this! Why would God let this happen? I hate you!
3. Bargaining — Maybe we can work this out.
4. Depression —This hurts too much. Why bother to go on?
5. Acceptance — It is what it is. Let's get on with it.

The stages can occur in different orders and they can even reoccur. Both men and women will experience these stages to some degree.

My message here is particularly for heterosexual women. While you are going through these stages, be mindful of getting involved with a "he-man woman hater." These are guys who are themselves often narcissists who deep down have a problem with women, likely from somewhere in their sick puppy past. Why else would a grown man take advantage of a woman who is coming out of a divorce in order to get what he wants sexually or financially, while giving little to nothing in return?

Many recently divorced women will go through a "crazy period," particularly if the breakup involved their husband being unfaithful. The woman feels a sense of rejection and that they somehow were no longer "good enough." The pain triggers within them a desire to get their groove back, which is often really about getting back at their ex-husband. The women doll themselves up to get back out on the dating market. They often make themselves overly available to be another man's treasure in a desire to convince themselves that they are not their ex-husband's trash. In reality, they become easy prey for the "he-man woman hater."

The "he-man woman hater" is the guy who will meet a wounded woman on, perhaps, a long airplane flight. They will strike up a conversation about where they are flying to, their careers, and then their families. The woman will share that she is divorcing or divorced and that it was ugly. The man may also be divorced or separated. During the long flight, she'll offer details about the painful breakup, because, being deeply into one of the above grief stages, she'll want a sympathetic ear. The "he-man woman hater" might share some of his breakup story, forming a common connection with the woman. Prior to landing, they will exchange phone numbers and then eventually rendezvous back in their home city. One thing will lead to the inevitable.

Instead of seeing that the woman is obviously hurt and needs to take a relationship break to assess her present and future, the "he-man woman hater" will instead think only about himself and his own desires. Since in her pain the woman will likely want to feel the physical touch of another man to mend her esteem, sense of value, she'll buy into the guys corny lines.

Women tend to have a hard time truly listening to what men actually say. Perhaps it is because women tend to be more idealistic. Meanwhile, women often (and correctly) complain that men typically don't communicate their true thoughts and feelings well. Research, such as by biological anthropologist Helen Fisher, shows that women and men both have the hormones estrogen and testosterone. People with high estrogen activity (typically females) tend to have superior verbal skills. They also tend to be emotionally expressive. Meanwhile, people with high testosterone activity (typically men) tend to be more analytical, while being emotionally restrained. Even if a man is a good communicator and clearly tells a woman that he is honestly not offering anything more than sex, she (especially if she is grieving her divorce) will likely *hear* that he is offering her the intimacy and love that she longs to regain. For a woman who missed her father's nurturing as a girl, it unearths an even deeper pain.

"He'll change," women tend to convince themselves.

Meanwhile, the "he-man woman hater" is often still licking wounds too. Perhaps it's from that first love in high school that broke his heart, or because he had difficulty getting dates when he was in college. Or because his ex-wife left him because he was immature and inadequate, or because she too had "daddy issues." Instead of recognizing that the woman is hurt (or perhaps suffering from a mental illness), the "he-man woman-hater" manipulates and takes what he wants. He strings the woman along, even to the point of borrowing money from her that he doesn't intend to return. He will take favors from her, like having her drive him around town in her car and not even pay for gas. Calling this narcissist a "dog" who will eventually "have his day" is actually a compliment. Such a man is really more like a puppy.

A mature wise man would have compassion and empathy for a woman who is grieving. For example, a married friend of mine told me that he was approached by a female college classmate who was divorcing. The two of them were taking an adult education course together at a local community college. The wounded woman would often wear low-cut blouses and would strategically position herself so that he couldn't help but notice her cleavage. One day, he happened to be out at a restaurant/bar with some friends and the woman came in alone. The establishment on Broadway Boulevard had a small dance floor. Upon seeing him, the classmate grabbed his hand saying, "Let's dance!" He paused, as he thought about his wife at home, but then obliged, thinking, *No harm, no foul.* While dancing, his friends let him know that they were leaving and waved goodbye. After dancing, my married friend and his female classmate returned to the table. She ordered a fresh drink and he was finishing his. As they talked, she revealed that her husband of several years finally admitted to her that he was gay.

"He wanted to finally be honest with himself after 10 years of marriage? Yeah, right," she said angrily.

"Well, I know that must have been tough to hear. I'm sorry that had to happen," my married friend replied.

"I appreciate you saying that," the woman said while gazing into his eyes.

Suddenly, she reached over the table and kissed my friend's lips. He paused, then pulled back.

"You know I'm married, right?" he said.

"And?" she replied.

"Well, this is not something that I need, nor is it something that you need at this time of your life," my friend responded calmly. "I appreciate your interest, and I do think that you are attractive, but I'm fine where I am. Besides, you can do much better. I respect you, so let this be good night and no more."

My friend said that he smiled as he rose from the table and left enough money to cover the drinks and the tip.

When a woman is obviously wounded and in that "divorce grief-crazy period," what prize is there to be gained by preying on her weaknesses? A mature man (a gentleman) would see that he would obviously be bringing more pain. The "he-man woman-hater" (especially a guy who is 30 or older and should know better) sees only personal—and primarily sexual—gain. Growing up I was very close to my late mother, even as our relationship evolved during my adult years. As I mentioned previously, I saw up close the pain she experienced after she and my father divorced. I have three older sisters, one of whom I was raised with and whom I remain very close with as well. I witnessed her relationship ups and downs. Both my mother and sister taught me a lot about how women think and feel. They instilled in me a healthy love for and respect of women. My daughter absolutely sealed that deal for me at her birth on through her evolution into the wonderful young woman that she has become. I am painfully aware that I can't be with her 24 hours a day, seven days a week, 365 days a year to protect her. Lord knows what I would do to someone who intentionally hurt my daughter, particularly if it were a sexual assault.

A man who would take advantage of a wounded, grieving divorcee is nothing more than a weak little boy. Women, when a "he-man woman hater" steps into your life, follow your gut and tell him to keep moving.

POSTSCRIPT

Before we leave this chapter, I thought I'd address one last thing: You are probably wondering about the identity of my daughter's biological father. Well, after weeks of prayer and contemplation, I put on my investigative journalist hat and began digging. My daughter granted me permission to do this on her behalf. I talked to several sources. These were, of course, difficult conversations, but as her dad I feel strongly that it would be better for me to take the hit than to have my daughter endure being hung up on or verbally abused. Out of respect for my daughter's privacy, I'll just leave it there. She knows the rest of the story. Whatever she decides to do (or not do) with the information that I uncovered, I will support her. I just want her to be healthy and at peace.

RECAP

Sometimes divorce is unavoidable and actually the best decision. Some marriages should never have happened, which is why an annulment is still necessary. However, the laws need to be updated to match our current 21st-century technologically advanced world. Like in my case, where an annullable offense actually occurred, you can understand why it is vital that you investigate your potential partner and yourself thoroughly before saying "I do." Listening to your gut will go a long way in leading you to the right decisions and hopefully a happy, lasting marriage. If you must divorce, try to remain calm, and get a good attorney to handle the case. I repeat, get a good attorney to look over everything before you sign. I made the irrational mistake of trusting a person that my gut had always told me I could not trust! Allowing your emotions to run amuck can lead to bad decisions that could scar your opportunity for post-marriage happiness. However, NEVER allow anyone to take your power from you or to steal your joy.

Throughout the courtroom ordeal, I managed to remain cool for the most part. However, there was a moment where I nearly lost it. Toward the end, the opposing attorney intentionally insulted me and my daughter. He referred to her as "buyer's remorse." He used the phrase twice. This was the view of the other side concerning my finding out that my daughter is not my biological child.

"He just doesn't want to pay," he told the judge.

My attorney must've felt my blood boil as I moved. He stood and objected angrily. Judge Jones just sat there gazing down. Apparently it was his view too.

Again, this is all in the court transcripts.

During a divorce, both men and women will likely go through a "crazy period" of uncharacteristic behavior. However, as a man, I warn women to be careful of the "he-man women haters" out there. These guys prey on wounded women. They slither around because they are often still weak little boys. Many people have been able to leave a marriage and quickly enter into another committed relationship or marriage successfully. Most should take time to heal from and even mourn the concluded marriage. Assess where you are and how you want your future to be. Then, allow it happen. Get out of your own way.

CHAPTER 9

ADVICE FROM MARRIAGE REALITY VETERANS

Dear Daughter,

As you date, I know that at some point you might be tempted to live with the guy. In fact, nowadays many people believe that deciding to live together exclusively is commitment enough, like a marriage. You will believe that you love him and that the two of you will eventually head down the marriage road when you are both ready. Besides, you'll figure that financially it makes sense to combine living expenses to save money, especially since you are both spending so much time together. This is one of the reasons people use as justification for "shackin' up," which I don't recommend. Shackin' is when there is no commitment timetable; you're both just "kickin' it" day to day. You are aware that your mother and I shack'd first. As a result, it seemed as if I backed into everything and was always reacting to circumstances.

True, living together can and has worked

out for many other couples, but I believe shackin' works particularly to the disadvantage of women in heterosexual relationships. Science shows that, biologically, women are more inclined to bond with their sex partner, while men are more about seeking pleasure. By shackin', the woman tends to give the man the access to the pleasure that he wants, while she doesn't necessarily get the bond she desires in return. With no legal document in hand, the most independent woman is bound to feel insecure eventually. And though the woman will try to mask her insecurity, it will likely seep out in various (and negative) ways.

Daughter, if you decide to live with the guy, it won't unleash Armageddon. It could work out for you, like it has for many truly committed couples. Just know that it likely won't reap the benefits that you hope for. It's often said that you don't really get to know a person until you actually live with them up close and personal. Actually, I know now that you often DO NOT get to know a person until you no longer live with them. When under the same roof, it can be harder to evaluate the relationship from a clear vantage point until you are ready to commit. Your vision blurs when you are too close to your cell phone screen, right? Blurred vision can lead you to ignore the deal-breaker signs and your gut instincts before you say "I do." That clearer vantage point beforehand—that distance provided by your own roof—can make the difference between marriage success and failure. It can heighten your desire for each other. It can also help you see that you're better off apart. If you decide to live together, start by at least being engaged to be married—that you are BOTH committed to a timetable and potential long-term life plan. Otherwise, you are just "playing house."

I'm a believer (and I know education experts back me up on this) that we learn best not when life is sweet, but when things have gone sour. Whatever the thing is, when it does not work as we planned, it leaves a marker that, if we're wise, causes us to evaluate why it didn't work. If we embrace shortfalls and process the reasons, we learn and become better for it. We know that we've learned because we do not repeat the same negative result.

Why did I write "shortfall" instead of "failure?" True, the definition of failure is that you did not achieve a particular goal. But when it comes to growing along life's journey, failure occurs only when you don't learn lessons from the previous experience to be applied to your next situation. This is probably at the root of why second marriages end at a higher rate (60 to 70 percent for heterosexual pairings) than first marriages. Third marriage divorce rates are even higher—about 74 percent. Now that's failure!

This chapter will offer advice from marriage veterans who are trying to get it right the second time around to help you avoid their fate. It will cover topics including why living together before getting married isn't smart, the importance of being honest from the start of your relationship, and why not everyone sees love and marriage the way that you do.

SHACKIN' IS NOT A RECOMMENDED TEST DRIVE

A daughter of a friend of mine moved in with her boyfriend after graduating from college and getting her first job. Her boyfriend already had the apartment, but had a roommate who moved out. Her moving in was to fill the financial shortfall and potentially set in motion what would eventually lead to the altar. Well, that's what she was thinking at least. As months turned to two years, there was still no marriage. My friend's daughter began complaining that her boyfriend was a poor communicator. Basically, she had provided him with the goods that he wanted out of the relationship without the down payment or certificate of deposit she desired. What incentive did he have to marry her? He had a roommate with benefits! Eventually, she became pregnant, though she honestly didn't intend to. Now an innocent child was being brought into the dysfunctional mix. Yeah, great idea.

A 2009 study from the University of Denver found that 19

percent of married couples who had shacked up before tying the knot had considered splitting, compared with 12 percent of couples who lived together after their engagement and 10 percent of couples who didn't live together at all before saying "I do." Apparently, there is something to be said for two people at least verbally committing to each other. Of course, shackin' may work just fine for many, but the statistics are not in the favor of shackers. Again, these are generalities. There are women who are not interested in bonding and there are men who are. There are married couples who first shacked up and are doing just fine. There are couples who have never married and have remained monogamous and committed to each other for years (such as in the case of many gay couples who, for so long this was their only choice in the United States, though this is changing). Because I have an opinion on this does not automatically make my opinion right for you. Again, couples should decide for themselves together what works best for them. However, I strongly suggest that you don't shack up for the reasons I previously stated. The odds and the karma are not in your favor.

According to the book, *7 Stages of Marriage: Laughter, Intimacy and Passion Today, Tomorrow, Forever* by therapist Rita M. DeMaria, Ph.D., and co-writer Sari Harrar, marriages typically go through the following periods: honeymoon/passion, realization, rebellion, cooperation, reunion, explosion, and completion. Bell said that when you live together before marriage, you basically bypass the honeymoon/passion stage and start at the realization stage. As you begin seeing that your spouse is human and potentially has deal-breaking habits, you're forced into defensive mode. "You immediately react to them, which triggers a counteraction. It's like juggling everything at once," she said. "You don't have as much space to retreat and analyze and reflect upon what you see in your spouse." If you had your own home, you could simply go there to retreat and reflect. You can regroup and become proactive. You can play offense. You also don't have the benefit of leftover passion from the honeymoon stage that you could draw from to inspire hope that your spouse is still worth living with, Bell said.

Couples who want to marry often live together as a way of collecting data to see if the marriage will work. However, along with premarital counseling, there are better ways to collect marriage prospect data to help you decide if you've got a deal breaker on your hands. For example, I believe that driving in a car together for at least 60 minutes to a place where neither of you is sure of can tell you a lot of about each other.

Live in Your Car Instead

The car is a perfect metaphor for a marriage relationship: You're in closed quarters, like living in a home. In a vehicle are two people heading in the same direction who will arrive together. On a long trip where you don't know the exact location you're going to, you will have to either work together to accomplish the trip, or one person has to trust the other to get both of you there. When you're driving, does your partner in the passenger seat kick back and relax, or are they nervously slamming their foot as if pressing on the brakes? When they are driving, do you relax, or do you try to tell them how to drive? Are you at peace? If not, why? What about the dynamics of being in a car with your partner and other people that you know? Does your behavior toward each other change? Pay attention to this. If you're alone in the car with your marriage prospect, you have to focus on each other only. Can you drive for more than an hour with no music playing and just talk? Try turning the music off and see how you vibe together.

A male friend of mine who was on a date shared that he actually had a very good driving experience with the woman he was with. They were in Washington, D.C., which with its N.W., S.W. directions and circular streets can be a nightmare for those who are from out of town. GPS has its obvious advantages, but it can be difficult to follow GPS while driving in a high traffic urban area and having to make many sharp turns. My male friend lives in Philadelphia and his date had grown up in Alexandria, Virginia, but had not lived in the area for years. After driving down I-95 and picking her up from Baltimore Washington Thurgood Marshall Airport, my friend told his date up front that he didn't like driving in D.C., so he was totally submitting himself to her directions because she was more familiar. She was tired from flying several hours from the Midwest, so she wasn't up to driving. She agreed to copilot but explained that she had forgotten a lot, so he should be patient. He agreed.

As they arrived in D.C. and drove to find a certain restaurant, traffic became heavy. She began advising him to detour down different streets to get to their location. "Turn down M Street," she said. "Oh, no. I don't think that was right. Sorry. I think we have to go to Constitution Avenue." This went on for another 20 minutes, but they were talking and listening to music in between. Nonetheless, what should have been about a 60 minute drive from the airport had become more than 90 minutes. She expressed concern to my friend that he might have been thinking she was a total ditz, but he told her that he was actually fine with the situation. He was enjoying her company. He had already agreed to be patient.

"We'll get there whenever we get there," he said.

Suddenly, she had to use the restroom, so they agreed to get back to a main street so that she could go into a store to use a public restroom. As she guided them back, she spotted a different restaurant to use the restroom.

"I'll circle the block or double park until you're ready," he said.

They planned to get back on the road to find the original restaurant they were looking for.

"You must be tired," she said. "How about we just eat here?"

"Sure, let's make it happen," he responded.

He parked at the valet, they went inside, and the rest of the evening was enjoyable.

The reason why this situation worked out is that they were up front and honest about their expectations and limitations. They were more focused on empathy and enjoying each other's company, so when the inconveniences came up, neither of them became uptight.

If you were in either of their seats, would you have blown your top? You can learn a lot in a car about how well you might get along with someone under the same roof.

Be Up Front With Each Other

A caller to my show acknowledged that he was a divorcé. He said that there were a lot of troubles in his marriage that could have been avoided and resolved but weren't because he and his wife were operating under certain myths. One of the myths is that a marriage is 50/50, he said. "It's 100/100," the caller explained. "If you only put in 50/50, you're going to come up 100 short!" He also warned that couples should not go into a marriage lying to one another. "He or she is going to believe that lie and the darkness is going to come to light at some point. It hurts both partners because one told a lie . . . 'Yeah I want to have kids, I want this or that' when in reality she didn't want to have children. She wanted to use you as a stepping stone to get to her program and vice versa . . . be upfront with each other."

Honesty is an absolute must in a marriage. It's about being upright, fair, and free from deceit. When you're free from deceit, this means you are transparent; you're not hiding anything. If you're going to walk a lifetime with someone, obviously at the very beginning of your journey, you want to be honest to set the tone for a successful life together. To begin the marriage with major lies means you will find yourself adding lies on top of lies on top of lies to keep the original lie hidden. Anyone who can lie to their marriage prospect about any major issue of the relationship clearly does not love that person.

Lying to protect your own self-interest at the expense of others is always unacceptable and foul, especially when it involves hurting people who love you. However, sometimes lying or withholding the truth IS necessary to protect an innocent loved one. Let's take for example a woman who was once a prostitute, but whose life changed after she bore a child from a client. Let's say the woman gets her life on track and along the way meets a good man. She tells him the truth about her past life and they marry while the child is a toddler. The man adopts the child. I can understand them withholding the truth from their child about the biological father because of the mother's past. I can see them waiting until the child is older, perhaps even an adult, to explain the truth. What would be the point of a child growing up knowing that their mom was a prostitute and that their father was one of her Johns, especially if that child has two loving and committed parents? If knowing the truth can damage an innocent child's psyche, then delaying the truth until they are older and can understand it more clearly could be a better option.

When you truly love someone, these are the types of complex

sacrifices and risks that are worth taking. Though there are exceptions, people who lie big in relationships rarely do so out of love for another person. It's usually done to advance their self-interests. Eventually, lies fester and, as I said previously, blow up in your face when you are least expecting them.

Your Love Might Not Be Like My Love

Another caller cited different notions of love as a key culprit that leads to a broken marriage later. The caller said, for example, that some people only know a physical love because of the type of upbringing they had. As children, they were never taught to love for reasons such as caring for and being committed to a person. People go into relationships assuming instead of communicating. They assume that the other person shares their idea of what love is—as if we all had the same family experience. The caller suggested that couples need to explore this together. "You don't have to agree, but have an openness to be willing to listen," she said.

What's your potential spouse's idea of love? Have a conversation with him or her and find out.

Take the First Exit Ramp

After my divorce, it didn't take very long for me to have the opportunity to test the advice that I lay out here in this book—embracing the wisdom of your gut and follow it. I met a woman at a gathering with family and friends. She is beautiful, educated, has a career, and is doing well financially. As we began talking, we took a liking to each other. She shared that she had divorced several years ago and that she was exiting her current relationship with her boyfriend. They were living separately, but had some joint financial obligations that they were trying to navigate amicably. Not *exactly* great signs initially, but not necessarily deal breakers either—so I thought. I kind of favor connecting with women who have some relationship battle scars, that is, if those scars are healed. Since they already know the pain of breaking up, it could mean less drama going forward, right?

Upon learning that I was recently divorced, the woman

commented that she didn't think marriage was in her future.

"My experience hasn't made me down and out on marriage," I said. "I think it's about taking your time and allowing yourself to connect with the right person."

I told her that after 20-plus years of matrimonial drama, I certainly was on a sabbatical for several years or more and wasn't eager to jump into another committed relationship. Still, as I dated, I wanted to primarily interact with women that I might potentially see myself being married to down the road. I'm focused on finishing my doctorate, career goals, planning for retirement, and enjoying life in the moment daily. I don't want or need a lot of drama and distractions. I have a clear idea of the type of woman I am compatible with, I said. Yet, I don't plan on being that guy in his late 60s in the restaurant, bingo hall, or on Facebook flirting as if I'm trying to recapture the past glory days of my roaring 20s.

I explained my position further by using a football game analogy.

"I'm not approaching relationships like I'm in my 20s, in the first or second quarter of my life—just playing the field aimlessly," I told her. "I'm coming out of the locker room fresh and wiser as I start the third quarter of my life. I can't afford to make any major relationship mistakes in the second half of this game. You can't always stick with the player(s) that you start the game with if you plan on finishing with a victory."

The *special, special friend* said that she understood—so it seemed. Both of us were in transition. Neither one of us was interested in marriage anytime soon because we both realized we needed a break from navigating the potentially too high expectations of commitment. We were both interested in enjoying each other's company based on the terms that we both agreed upon. Low expectations, low drama and stress, right?

Our follow-up phone conversations were great, which led to more in-person meetings. As we shared more, our guards lowered more. We were both collecting data for future analysis at the appropriate time. However, we were both also free to date other people. I shared my career plans and goals after finishing my doctorate and that I particularly wanted to get back to writing more books. She was extremely supportive and encouraging.

She shared her aspirations, including running her own business at some point. I loved that idea as well.

During other casual conversation moments, she would sometimes (as women tend to do) make negative comments about her body. She said that her backside was a bit bigger and flatter than she wanted it to be. She joked that she might have a procedure to suck away a few inches of belly fat.

"Would you still like me if I got a boob job?" she quipped, revealing a beautiful smile and sparkling eyes.

"Hey, if you must," I joked back. "If that's what you want, but if you're serious, don't keep talking about it, though."

Reading in between the lines and connecting dots from informational moments like these is a vital way of getting to learn a person. You certainly won't get their full story in one long sitting over dinner or at a theater during a play. You have to read a person while they are consciously, but more importantly, *unconsciously* communicating. A paragraph gleaned here and there eventually gives you enough data to run a report or construct a chapter that tells a significant story. Over the course of a few months, there were several moments of seemingly innocent, yet revealing conversations and observations. Certainly there were things that I said and did (positive and negative) that she observed and that were duly noted on her end as well. Once while we were relaxing and watching a funny movie on TV, she said out of the blue, "I notice you don't curse or get angry much." I guess a scene in the movie triggered her thought.

Still, despite what I observed, I was just collecting data, not judging or analyzing. No mental reports were being run or storylines formed. I knew I was only hearing her side of her relationship story regarding her "ex" to whom she still had curious ties. Remember, I'm on SABBATICAL. Apparently, this wasn't how she was approaching things. She *was* in data analysis mode.

One day, my *special, special friend* called me unexpectedly while I was working on my dissertation. Our phone conversation took a very odd turn, though. She was talking to me while driving in her car—circling her neighborhood before stopping at her home. She said that she was at a major crossroads in her life. She had taken on a new job. She was having trouble grasping why she had not totally *severed* the relationship with her *ex-boyfriend*. She wasn't sure that "jumping into a relationship with me" was the right move.

"I'm not sure that I'm cut out for marriage and I'm seeing a pattern of my love life and I'm trying to follow my gut like we've both been saying and you're a relationship person who needs certain things, and you're a great guy, but I don't think you're the one for me . . . " she rambled.

And then I heard the old classic cliché, "But it's not you. It's me . . . "

"Hold it, hold it, hold it," I said, cutting her off abruptly. "Marriage? Marriage? Who said anything about marriage? And I haven't heard that old 'You're not the problem, the problem is me' line since I used it several times when I was in my 20s and even back in high school breaking up with a girl."

There was silence on the other end.

"Look, don't start doing my thinking for me," I said. "I'm very good at thinking and communicating for myself."

I proceeded to remind her of what I had said from the outset—that I was on SABBATICAL and not looking to immediately jump into another committed relationship. I only wanted to date women who I thought from the outset *might* have marriage potential. I had learned from my first and only un-merry-go-'round that dating a person without seriously considering whether they have marriage potential is a bad idea. Suddenly you start living together and then one thing often leads to another. Then, you find yourself perhaps pregnant and asking, "How did I get here long-term?" Why bother spending valuable time dating someone who you can't begin seeing yourself with long-term? There is a difference between being open to marriage some day and looking to marry tomorrow.

"I didn't say I wanted you to leave the guy you call your ex-boyfriend so that I could put a ring on your finger next," I said. "If you truly want to sever ties, good for you, but that's up to the two of you. Maybe I wasn't clear, but I thought I had been consistent with that. If you want to go a different direction in our friendship, I'm fine with that. But why are you blindsiding me with this over the phone? Couldn't we have discussed this in person on any of the several occasions we've been together? Surely you didn't just wake up yesterday to this revelation, right?"

She confirmed that I had been consistent with my position and that hearing it again had made it clearer to her. (Didn't I write previously that women have a tendency to not *truly* listen well to men? They tend to hear what men say, but interpret it in ways that fit the woman's preset thoughts?) As the cell phone tension subsided, we hung up laughing and remained on good terms. We agreed to let the universe handle our friendship naturally.

The message I received from the GPS was clear—when someone cares enough about you to show you an exit ramp from their highway, take it. Re-route because there is likely much more going on with them that they do NOT want you to discover. The person is likely warning you that a collision is up ahead. There are always three sides to a story, especially a love story. Like balancing a coin, the truth is typically found along the narrow edge because you can see all sides clearly. A wobbly coin is a sign that the relationship may be too costly when it eventually drops on either heads or tails.

So I took the exit ramp before paying the toll.

This encounter caused me to more deeply reevaluate my own patterns of dating and "romantic drama" from even as far back as college. Why? The common denominator in these relationships is ME, so just *maybe* that's where the problem truly is, right? Why have so many of my lady friends been in the process of "exiting" relationships? Do I find this appealing? Do I subconsciously figure that since they're still technically "attached" to someone that they won't want to quickly latch on to me? The chain, lock and key happened anyway. I was the so-called "greener grass." However, in those relationships, we both ended up behaving badly; they eventually left for what they believed was a better patch of greener grass. Perhaps I should deal only with women who have exited and shut the door on any ideas of returning. Woman who are unequivocally unattached. What a novel idea!

While on relationship sabbatical I would explore this more thoroughly. Love relationships and who you will or won't end up with are hard to predict. However, patterns of your own behavior unveil tendencies that can reveal predictable outcomes.

RECAP

Take it from me, a marriage reality veteran, shackin' as a test drive isn't a smart move for most women. You each are likely to give up too much of yourselves without getting back what you desire. You're not likely to learn any more about the person that would assure you that marriage is the right move. Or, you could end up backing your way into an ill-advised marriage. If you do live together, get engaged. You can both still say, "I don't" later. Also, dishonesty at the start and throughout a relationship and marriage is dumb and dangerous. You will have to keep up with your lies and eventually you will slip and forget what you've already said. In the end, the truth will come to light and, sadly, innocent people (perhaps children) will be the collateral damage long term. Lastly, believing that everyone sees love and marriage the way that you do is naïve. We all have different experiences, even if we share similar backgrounds. Don't go into a relationship making assumptions that the other person already understands where you are coming from. Communicate openly, honestly and frequently to get on the same page BEFORE you say "I do." Even if you're not driving toward marriage yet, don't be afraid to take the first "exit ramp" if you see signs in a relationship that a dead-end or collision may be up ahead.

CHAPTER 10

QUIZ: ARE YOU READY FOR MARRIAGE?

As I stated earlier, fathers are key to giving daughters a positive sense of identity, self-love and security that they will need as women and potentially wives and mothers. *Dear Daughter* illustrates the type of pain-saving wisdom that many women miss out on when their father/daughter relationship is broken or nonexistent. When a father fails to pass these keys on to his daughter, and if the daughter in turn fails to take accountability for her "daddy issues" and actions as an adult woman, she WILL lash out at her husband. If she becomes a mother, she WILL pass down her pain to her own children, particularly her daughter.

Plenty of healthy and successful adults were raised by good single parents. Marriage remains the ideal relationship under which children are often born and raised. There are several keys to unleashing and maintaining a happy marriage. The master key has to be that from the outset you make the right choice for the right reasons. The key to making the right choice is to clearly know yourself and what you want in a spouse. You should be able to articulate it or even write it down. Then you can toss it out into the universe so that your desire will come back to you. Rather than tell yourself, "I don't ever want a man who is like my father," gravitate toward people who have characteristics that you DO like in your father. If not your father, model another positive male from your upbringing. If you back away from what you don't want, you will end up backing into it anyway because you won't see where you are going. Your wounded subconscious mind will call the shots with its old familiar patterns. How do you know if a person is right for you? How do you know that you're ready? Do not, do not, and do not ignore the warning signs. You've got to follow your gut instincts. The following quiz could help you decide if you're ready to marry and if the person you're thinking of tying the knot with is "the one."

QUESTIONS

1. Do you believe your marriage prospect is your equal in several significant ways (ex: intellect, appearance, financially)?

2. When you hear the word "submit," do you think it means to be subservient?

3. Do you think having a disagreement where you are yelling angrily at each other is OK?

4. Would it be OK to make major decisions that significantly impact your spouse without their knowledge and input?

5. When your mate is not present, do you act in ways (flirt) that you would not if your mate were around?

6. Do you believe your marriage prospect needs you?

7. Would you be willing to make all of your financial information available to your spouse?

8. Do you and your marriage prospect share the same family values (ex: raising children, valuing education, spirituality)?

9. Are you as comfortable telling your marriage prospect about your past as you are in knowing about theirs?

10. If a particular thing about your marriage prospect (smoker, clingy, jealous, jobless, moody, poor communicator) that rubs you the wrong way NOW was to never change, could you deal with it forever?

11. If you are in an interracial relationship, do you believe that your marriage prospect is an exception to the rule of the negative stereotype of their racial or ethnic group or nationality?

12. Would you be uncomfortable with your children spending a lot of time with your spouse's family members (parents, siblings, cousins, etc.)?

13. Is it OK to lie to your spouse about major issues that would have an impact on him or her?

14. Would you be OK if your spouse made more money than you?

15. Would you be OK if YOU made more money than your spouse?

16. Are you and your marriage prospect in agreement on whether to have children and how many?

17. Would you be willing to adopt children if your marriage prospect wants to?

18. Do you believe your marriage prospect would never do anything to hurt you?

19. Do you think it would be acceptable to have sexual affairs behind your spouse's back?

20. If your spouse were to achieve success at their goals, would you feel that they owe you something?

ANSWERS

1. **Yes**. The person who looks down upon and belittles another human being typically does so because they themselves feel inadequate.

2. **No.** Submitting doesn't make you a slave or weak. It actually takes a stronger person to yield to their partner when it is in the best interest of the family and the relationship.

3. **No.** Most arguments have nothing to do with what you're arguing about. Exploding because the toilet seat was left up is probably more about feeling someone is inconsiderate. Yelling is about a struggle for power. If you have each other's best interest at heart, there's no reason to attack each other.

4. **No.** So you would take that new job that requires you to relocate across the country without consulting with your spouse? Yes, you are still an individual, but as a spouse, you've signed on to be a team player. So play team ball! Empower each other to make executive decisions, but consult each other on big decisions.

5. **No.** What is done in the dark will come to light, especially nowadays where people have cameras on their phones and will post photos on social media. If you are being a chameleon, this is probably a sign that you or your spouse will have sexual intimacy problems.

6. **No.** Your marriage prospect should "want" you, not need you. Trust me, you don't want to be a codependent that is with a dependent or vice versa.

7. **Yes.** You work hard for your money, but when you're married you become a joint venture, a team. Even if you agree to sign a prenuptial agreement, be transparent with each other about your financial worth.

8. **Yes.** If you all butt heads over such things as whether the children should attend private school, you will feel as though you are sleeping with the enemy. You don't have to agree on everything, but if you are not on the same page regarding basic beliefs, then God help you!

9. **Yes.** This is actually more about honest communication and trust—particularly if you don't like being blindsided—then it is about being nosy. Don't ask about their past if you're not willing to be honest about your own. And definitely don't ask what you can't handle.

10. **Yes.** If your answer is no, then you should immediately drop the idea of marrying the person and just remain friends. YOU can't "fix" them and YOU have no right to! If you plow through with the marriage anyway, you will be setting up yourself and your spouse for years and years of frustration and a likely divorce.

11. **No.** Putting your marriage prospect on a pedestal and saying things such as, "You're different from the rest of your people," still indicates that you have some bigoted attitudes toward your potential spouse. If you have children, those attitudes would transfer to them also.

12. **No.** When you marry a person, you also marry their family, the community of loved ones who helped to produce them. These people could be an important support system, like the African proverb that says, "It takes a village to raise a child." If you reject your marriage prospect's family, you are also potentially rejecting an important part of their identity. The key is to have appropriate boundaries with family members. What you do not want is an enmeshed family, where people do not understand boundaries, such as respecting the values you want to instill in your children.

13. **No.** It is never OK to lie about anything major that would negatively affect the person you love and with whom you plan to spend your life. Put everything on the table or the lie

will eventually come to light and blow up in your face when you least expect it.

14. **Yes.** Some men and women believe that the man should ALWAYS make more money than the woman. Or there might be the assumption that one partner is more dominant (perhaps because they are more educated or skilled), so they should always have the dominant income to match. You should discuss this issue honestly. As the economy tightens and competition for jobs toughens, it is no longer guaranteed that one person will ALWAYS be the main breadwinner.

15. **Yes.** Some men and women believe that the man should ALWAYS make more money than the woman, but many women have embraced the idea that they can bring home the bacon and cook it. If you would be uncomfortable earning more than your spouse, discuss a contingency plan together now of what you both would do in case this happens.

16. **Yes.** The rearing of children is traditionally one of the key reasons why people marry. However, even some young couples of childbearing age are not interested in having children. Make sure you both agree on whether to have children or not. And if so, how many.

17. **Yes.** Some couples see the need to parent children who have already been born and would love to have a happy home. Sometimes couples discover that they are unable to conceive. Adoption is a highly recommended viable option. But if one of you would not be willing to do it, then you might have a deal-breaker on your hands.

18. **No.** People are human. You can count on human beings to disappoint and to hurt one another. It is best for you to think of the worst possible thing (short of murder) that your marriage prospect could do to you while you are married and realize that THEY COULD DEFINITELY DO IT! How do you know this is a certainty? Because YOU ARE HUMAN and under the right circumstances, YOU are capable of

justifying your behavior and doing something unimaginable to the person that you say that you love. During marriage, you should prepare for the worst, but behave toward your spouse in a way that is likely to bring out the best in them and you. Remember the power of empathy! You can only control yourself. You can't control what they do, so don't bother worrying. If you are overly worried, you are probably the one who is hiding and feeling guilty about something hurtful that you've done or are planning to do.

19. **No.** Trust me, infidelity is bad, which is why it is grounds for divorce. It deteriorates and breaks trust. It creates negative karma, which you eventually won't be able to rationalize or negotiate your way out of. If you are going to be with someone, *be with them!* Dipping outside signals a deeper intimacy problem.

20. **No.** If you and your spouse are one, then their success would mean that you also have achieved success. So why would you feel that they owe you something? You should team together to make sure that your individual and collective goals are aligned and that you are both being fulfilled. Your life should not be totally wrapped up and dependent upon your spouse and vice versa. If you are supporting each other and mutually benefitting each other, then their success—whether individual or collective—is your success. Your success—whether individual or collective—is their success.

*__18-20__ questions answered correctly—Congratulations, you are ready to get married!

*__13-17__ questions answered correctly—You're getting close to being ready, but additional talks with your spouse-to-be and premarital counseling sessions are in order.

*__12 or fewer questions answered correctly__—You're not ready for marriage. You still need to unpack your luggage. See a counselor to figure yourself out. Hang in there. The fact that you've read this book already means you're on the right track.

CONCLUSION

At the beginning of this book I revealed that during my divorce I discovered that my daughter is not my biological child. I shared that broken father/daughter relationships are often the root of "daddy issues" that sour our love relationships. We pass on the pain from parent to child, from generation to generation. I aim to continue doing my part as a father to empower my daughter (and sons) to break the chain.

I told you that a "technically" divorced heterosexual man could definitely deliver some valuable insights regarding how to have a successful marriage. I've been able to do that here because I'm not bitter about marriage. I believe in the institution. Had I not gone through my journey (it continues), I may not have ever uncovered some very important personal truths, including my own "daddy issues" linked to my parents' divorce; that I was a codependent . . . that I have that "needy gene."

Old behavior patterns and familiar habits can be hard to break. In a relationship it takes two willing minds that are committed to being honest and transparent about their luggage for a relationship to heal and thrive. My conscious and subconscious are no longer at odds, but are reading from the same playbook now:

I don't have a right to fix anyone, so I don't try.

"Making a marriage work" never works, particularly a marriage that is based on past dirty luggage and painful secrets. Unpack first!

Embrace that the past *is* present, but don't dwell on what can't be undone. Live in the present moment of the relationship always. The only moment I can change is now, so just "let it work."

Since I was only "technically" married in that I should have been able to get an annulment, I've decided that my next marriage will officially be my first. The woman that I connect with will be independent and self-assured. She will be the beneficiary of my personal journey to better understanding my forever growing self. The Law of Attraction being what it is, I'm confident in God's universe that the true bond will happen when we're both ready. If it doesn't, that's fine too.

As for my daughter, she encourages me, others and herself through her pain. She's one of the strongest and most caring people that I know. She is a born cheerleader. The truth that we are not biologically connected has been gut-wrenching for us both. But as she said in a poem that she wrote for me and performed on my birthday during an open-mic set at a lounge near our apartment, our love is "thicker and stronger than blood." My eyes welled with tears of joy that evening. She confirmed again that I had done the right thing in pursuing the truth despite the painful costs. She confirmed for me again the joy that I felt the day she was born—that God had chosen me to be her earthly daddy.

A successful marriage team hinges neither on being the coach who tells a player what to do nor the star player who might crave narcissistic attention. Cheerleaders are what spouses need to be for each other to sustain years of happiness—someone who will stand at your sideline no matter what the score is, be honest with you, and always root for you to win. Sons may make their fathers proud, but daughters often show daddies how to love. Good daddies model for them whom they should give their love to. If my daughter chooses to say, "I do," I look forward to walking her down the aisle someday. I plan to proudly give her hand over to the husband who, in his own unique and empathetic way, would cherish, appreciate and love my daughter as an equal partner in the godly way that she deserves to be.

ACKNOWLEDGMENTS

Though I pray that my sons also benefit from what I've written here, I dedicate this book to my daughter—my baby girl. Our bond has become stronger amid the deep pain that we have had to endure together and alone. Nonetheless, I am thankful for the joy and hope that I have through the pain. Tremendous thanks to my tight circle of family, friends and colleagues who have given their love and support. God has blessed me with a great support system.

www.ingramcontent.com/pod-product-compliance
Lightning Source LLC
Chambersburg PA
CBHW070143080526
44586CB00015B/1821